CUTE CROCHETED PLANTS

25 LOVABLE CROCHET DESIGNS!

EMMA VARNAM

CONTENTS

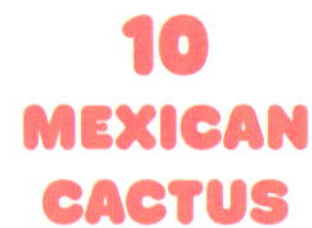

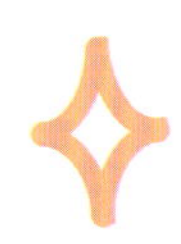

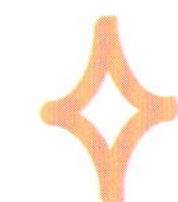

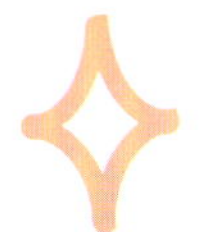

INTRODUCTION

I can't quite believe it, but this is my fourth plant-related crochet book! I can vividly remember making my first crocheted cactus. That autumn we had travelled to South Africa, and I had seen many succulents that are available as houseplants here in Britain. But there, the cacti and succulents are in their natural habitat, and they grow in abundance and to an enormous size. It was this sense of scale that switched on something in my brain. The very regular form reminded me of the structure of amigurumi, and I knew I would spend some time noodling with yarn to create a crochet version. Not long after, my first plant book, *Crocheted Succulents*, was born.

Since then I have created many woolly houseplants and flowers. It is a joy to think of all the ways you can take a strand of wool and a hook and try and make a natural thing. Often on a weekend or on holiday, a little thought enters my head and I think, 'Wouldn't it be fun to make a plant for a friend?' And that is how moments of creative whimsy begin. It quite literally is my one and only superpower.

Honestly, I have had such a great time making these patterns! You should feel very sorry for my poor family and friends who get sent endless photos with the caption, 'Isn't this hilarious?' whenever I come up with a new idea.

In recent years I have enjoyed designing *kawaii* items, a Japanese style of creating lovable and cute characters out of everyday objects or animals, which is where this book comes in. You can simplify a design and create a vibrant and expressive plant or flower. The key thing is to place the eyes and the embroidered faces in the right places, and it is a lot of fun when you get going. But most important of all is to stretch your imagination and enjoy the process. Change the colours, alter the expressions and put together a garden of delight that will never need watering or repotting.

Emma

THE
PLANTS

OPEN

MEXICAN CACTUS

A sassy succulent that reminds us of all those majestic cacti in the desert. The great thing is that you can't overwater this little chap!

YOU WILL NEED

- **Scheepjes Metropolis, 75% wool, 25% nylon (219yd/200m per 50g ball): 1 x 50g ball in 032 Abu Dhabi (A)**
- **Scheepjes Catona, 100% cotton (27yd/25m per 10g ball): 1 x 10g ball in 281 Tangerine (B)**
- **Stylecraft Special DK, 100% acrylic (323yd/295m per 100g ball): A small amount of 1054 Walnut (C)**
- **3mm (UK 11:US –) crochet hook**
- **3.5mm (UK 9:US E/4) crochet hook**
- **Tapestry needle**
- **Small bag of rice or lentils**
- **Polyester stuffing**
- **A strand of white and black yarn**
- **2 x ⅛in (4mm) black safety eyes**

NOTE

The cactus is worked in spirals using the standard amigurumi technique. You later sew small crosses onto the crochet fabric.

FINISHED SIZE

The cactus is approximately 3½in (9cm) tall and 1¾in (4cm) wide.

TECHNIQUES

Magic ring	Double crochet (dc)
Chain (ch)	dc2inc
Slip stitch (sl st)	dc2tog

LARGE LEAF

Using 3mm hook and A, make a magic ring.
Round 1: 1 ch, 6 dc into the centre of the ring.
Round 2: 2 dc into each st (12 sts).
Round 3: (1 dc, dc2inc) 6 times (18 sts).
Round 4: (2 dc, dc2inc) 6 times (24 sts).
Round 5: (11 dc, dc2inc) twice (26 sts).
Rounds 6–7: Work 2 rounds straight.
Round 8: (12 dc, dc2inc) twice (28 sts).
Rounds 9–15: Work 7 rounds straight.
Round 16: (12 dc, dc2tog) twice (26 sts).
Round 17: Work 1 round straight.
Round 18: (11 dc, dc2tog) twice (24 sts).
Round 19: Work 1 round straight.
Round 20: (10 dc, dc2tog) twice (22 sts).
Round 21: Work 1 round straight.
Fasten off. Leave a yarn tail to sew to the soil.

SMALL LEAF

Using 3mm hook and A, make a magic ring.
Round 1: 1 ch, 6 dc into the centre of the ring.
Round 2: 2 dc into each st (12 sts).
Rounds 3–7: Work 5 rounds straight.
Round 8: (4 dc, dc2tog) twice (10 sts).
Fasten off. Leave a yarn tail to sew to the large leaf.

FLOWER

Using 3mm hook and B, make a magic ring.
Round 1: 2 ch, 4 tr into the centre of the ring. Sl st into 2nd chain.
Fasten off and leave a tail of yarn.

SOIL

Using 3.5mm hook and C, make a magic ring.
Round 1: 1 ch, 6 dc into the centre of the ring.
Round 2: 2 dc into each st (12 sts).
Round 3: (1 dc, dc2inc) 6 times (18 sts).
Round 4: (2 dc, dc2inc) 6 times (24 sts).
Round 5: (3 dc, dc2inc) 6 times (30 sts).
Round 6: (4 dc, dc2inc) 6 times (36 sts).
Rounds 7–11: Work 5 rounds straight.
Round 12: (4 dc, dc2tog) 6 times (30 sts).
Round 13: (3 dc, dc2tog) 6 times (24 sts).
Round 14: (2 dc, dc2tog) 6 times (18 sts).
Place a small bag of rice or lentils in the base and then stuff firmly with polyester stuffing.
Round 15: (1 dc, dc2tog) 6 times (12 sts).
Round 16: (Dc2tog) 6 times (6 sts).
Using a tapestry needle, weave the yarn through the last dc sts of the round and gather hole together. Fasten off and weave in ends.

MAKING UP

Flatten each leaf with the palm of your hand. Using some white yarn, sew some small cross stitches to the surface of each leaf. Using the photograph as a guide, place the plastic eyes and stitch the mouth on the face using black yarn.

Sew the flower to the edge of the small leaf. Sew the small leaf to the edge of the large leaf. Put a little stuffing in the large leaf but leave it mainly flat. Using the tails of yarn, sew firmly to the soil.

Place into a small pot.

RED SUCCULENT

Succulents can come in such pretty and surprising colours. You can make this in any colour you choose, but this plant in a pot almost appears to have funky red hair.

YOU WILL NEED

- Scheepjes Catona, 100% cotton (137yd/125m per 50g ball): 1 x 50g ball in 517 Ruby (A)
- Stylecraft Special DK, 100% acrylic (323yd/295m per 100g ball): A small amount of 1064 Mocha (B) and 1054 Walnut (C)
- 3.5mm (UK 9:US E/4) crochet hook
- Tapestry needle
- Polyester stuffing
- A small piece of cardboard
- 2 x ⅜in (10mm) black safety eyes
- A strand of black yarn

FINISHED SIZE

The succulent is approximately 5in (12.5cm) in diameter.

TECHNIQUES

Magic ring
Chain (ch)
Slip stitch (sl st)
Double crochet (dc)
dc2inc
dc2tog
Half treble (htr)
Double treble (dtr)
Through back loop only (blo)

NOTE

The succulent is made of individual leaves which you position on a circle of brown soil. This is then sewn on the top of the pot.

LARGE LEAF (MAKE 5)

Using 3.5mm hook and A, make a magic ring.

Round 1: 1 ch, 4 dc into the centre of the ring.

Round 2: (Dc2inc) 4 times (8 sts).

Round 3: (3 dc, dc2inc) twice (10 sts).

Round 4: (4 dc, dc2inc) twice (12 sts).

Round 5: (5 dc, dc2inc) twice (14 sts).

Round 6: (6 dc, dc2inc) twice (16 sts).

Rounds 7–8: Work 2 rounds straight.

Round 9: (1 dc, dc2tog) 5 times, 1 dc (11 sts).

Round 10: (Dc2tog) 5 times, 1 dc (6 sts).

Fasten off and leave a tail of yarn.

SMALL LEAF (MAKE 4)

Using 3.5mm hook and A, make a magic ring.

Round 1: 1 ch, 4 dc into the centre of the ring.

Round 2: (Dc2inc) 4 times (8 sts).

Round 3: (3 dc, dc2inc) twice (10 sts).

Round 4: (4 dc, dc2inc) twice (12 sts).

Rounds 5–6: Work 2 rounds straight.

Round 7: (1 dc, dc2tog) 4 times (8 sts).

Round 8: (Dc2tog) 4 times (4 sts).

Fasten off and leave a tail of yarn.

CENTRE LEAF

Using 3.5mm hook and A, make a magic ring.

Round 1: 1 ch, 6 dc into the centre of the ring, join with a sl st.

Round 2: *(1 htr, 1 tr, 1 dtr, 1 tr, 1 htr) in next dc, sl st in next dc; rep from * twice (3 petals).

Fasten off and leave a tail of yarn.

POT

Using 3.5mm hook and B, make a magic ring.

Round 1: 1 ch, 8 dc into the centre of the ring.

Round 2: 2 dc into each st (16 sts).

Round 3: (1 dc, dc2inc) 8 times (24 sts).

Round 4: (2 dc, dc2inc) 8 times (32 sts).

Round 5: Work 1 round (32 sts).

Round 6: Work 1 round blo (32 sts).

Rounds 7–9: Work 3 rounds straight.

Round 10: (3 dc, dc2inc) 8 times (40 sts).

Rounds 11–12: Work 2 rounds straight.

Round 13: (4 dc, dc2inc) 8 times (48 sts).

Rounds 14–18: Work 5 rounds straight.

Rounds 19–20: Work 2 rounds blo (48 sts).

Round 21: 1 htr in each st (48 sts).

Round 22: Work 1 round blo (48 sts).

Fasten off and weave in ends.

SOIL TOP

Using 3.5mm hook and C, make a magic ring.

Round 1: 1 ch, 8 dc into the centre of the ring, join with a sl st.

Round 2: (Dc2inc) 8 times (16 sts).

Round 3: (1 dc, dc2inc) 8 times (24 sts).

Round 4: (2 dc, dc2inc) 8 times (32 sts).

Round 5: (3 dc, dc2inc) 8 times (40 sts).

Round 6: (4 dc, dc2inc) 8 times (48 sts).

Round 7: Work 1 round straight.

Fasten off and leave a long tail of yarn.

MAKING UP

Using the photograph as a guide, place the plastic eyes and stitch the mouth using black yarn. Place a small piece of cardboard (around 2¼in/6cm in diameter) in the base of the pot. Firmly stuff the pot. Fold the last two rounds of the pot over. Place the soil top on top and whip stitch (see page 122) the last rounds of the pot and the soil together.

Fold each leaf in half and press it flat with your hand. Arrange five large leaves to form a star, and, using the tail of yarn, sew the end rows together to form a flat star. Sew another star of four small leaves. Sew one star of leaves on top of the other, making sure the leaves overlap. Finally, sew the three small centre leaves right in the middle. Sew the base of the plant to the centre of the soil.

TROPICAL TALL CACTUS

The classic ribbed cactus is wearing a jaunty little flower and will look very cheeky hidden among your other house plants.

NOTE

The cactus is worked in rows. The rib is created by working into the back loop of each stitch (see page 118).

YOU WILL NEED

- **Drops Nord 4ply, 45% alpaca, 30% polyamide, 25% wool (186yd/170m per 50g ball): 1 x 50g ball in 19 Forest Green (A)**
- **Scheepjes Catona, 100% cotton (27yd/25m per 10g ball): 1 x 10g ball in 114 Shocking Pink (B)**
- **Stylecraft Special DK, 100% acrylic (323yd/295m per 100g ball): A small amount of 1054 Walnut (C)**
- **3mm (UK 11:US –) crochet hook**
- **3.5mm (UK 9:US E/4) crochet hook**
- **Tapestry needle**
- **Small bag of rice or lentils**
- **Polyester stuffing**
- **A strand of black yarn**
- **2 x ⅛in (4mm) black safety eyes**

FINISHED SIZE

The cactus is approximately 4in (10cm) tall and 2in (5cm) in diameter.

TECHNIQUES

Magic ring	dc2inc
Chain (ch)	dc2tog
Slip stitch (sl st)	Through back loop
Double crochet (dc)	only (blo)

CACTUS

Row 1: Using 3.5mm hook and A, ch 21 sts.
Row 2 WS: 1 dc in 2nd ch from hook, dc into each ch to end, turn (20 sts).
Rows 3–6: Work 4 rows straight, turn.
Row 7: 1 ch, dc blo into each st to end, turn (20 sts).
Rows 8–12: Work 5 rows straight, turn.
Rows 7–12 form the pattern. Rep pattern 5 times.
With RS together, now crochet the first and last rows together:
Next row: 1 ch, sl st in every st.
Fasten off and leave a long tail of yarn.

SPIKY FLOWER

Using 3mm hook and B, make a magic ring.
Round 1: 1 ch, 9 dc into the centre of the ring, join with a sl st.
Round 2: 6 ch, miss 1 ch, sl st along the rest of ch sts, sl st in same dc, * sl st in next st, 6 ch, miss 1 ch, sl st along the rest of ch sts, sl st in same dc; rep from * 7 times, sl st to join (9 petals).
Fasten off and leave a tail of yarn.

SOIL

Using 3.5mm hook and C, make a magic ring.

Round 1: 1 ch, 6 dc into the centre of the ring.

Round 2: 2 dc into each st (12 sts).

Round 3: (1 dc, dc2inc) 6 times (18 sts).

Round 4: (2 dc, dc2inc) 6 times (24 sts).

Round 5: (3 dc, dc2inc) 6 times (30 sts).

Round 6: (4 dc, dc2inc) 6 times (36 sts).

Rounds 7–11: Work 5 rounds straight.

Round 12: (4 dc, dc2tog) 6 times (30 sts).

Round 13: (3 dc, dc2tog) 6 times (24 sts).

Round 14: (2 dc, dc2tog) 6 times (18 sts).

Place a small bag of rice or lentils in the base and then stuff firmly with polyester stuffing.

Round 15: (1 dc, dc2tog) 6 times (12 sts).

Round 16: (Dc2tog) 6 times (6 sts).

Using a tapestry needle, weave this yarn through the last dc sts of the round and gather hole together. Fasten off and weave in ends.

MAKING UP

Using the photograph as a guide, place safety eyes and sew mouth using a strand of black yarn.

Gather together the stitches on one of the open ends to form the top of the cactus. Firmly stuff the cactus. Sew the pink flower to the top of the cactus. Then sew the open side of the cactus firmly to the soil.

Place into a small pot (see pages 124–5).

MINI FURRY CACTUS

Some of the tiny spiky cacti look so furry and cute that you want to give them a little stroke, but in reality they have lots of little spikes. You can touch this one as much as you like, as its furry halo is made of soft merino.

YOU WILL NEED

- **King Cole Merino Blend 4ply, 100% superwash wool (197yds/180m per 50g ball): 1 x 50g ball in 3941 Conifer (A)**
- **Drops Kid Silk, 75% mohair, 25% silk (230yds/210m per 25g ball): 1 x 50g ball in 01 Off White (B)**
- **Scheepjes Merino Soft, 50% wool, 25% microfibre, 25% acrylic (115yd/105m per 50g ball): 1 x 50g ball in 607 Braque (C)**
- **3.5mm (UK 9:US E/4) crochet hook**
- **Tapestry needle**
- **Polyester stuffing**
- **2 x ⅛in (4mm) safety eyes**
- **Strand of pink yarn**

FINISHED SIZE

Large cactus is approximately 2in (5cm) in diameter. Small cactus is approximately ¾in (2cm) in diameter.

TECHNIQUES

Magic ring	**Double crochet (dc)**
Chain (ch)	**dc2inc**
Slip stitch (sl st)	**dc2tog**

NOTE

The cacti are worked in spirals using the standard amigurumi technique. You then sew them together to create the whole plant.

SMALL CACTUS

Using 3.5mm hook and A, make a magic ring.

Round 1: 1 ch, 6 dc into the centre of the ring.
Round 2: 2 dc into each st (12 sts).
Round 3: (1 dc, dc2inc) 6 times (18 sts).
Round 4: (2 dc, dc2inc) 6 times (24 sts).
Rounds 5–9: Work 5 rounds straight.
Round 10: (2 dc, dc2tog) 6 times (18 sts).
Round 11: (1 dc, dc2tog) 6 times (12 sts).
Stop at this point. Put a safety pin on your working loop. Using the photograph as a guide, position and secure safety eyes on the cactus. Stuff firmly. Then return to finishing the decreasing, putting the working loop back on your crochet hook.
Round 12: (Dc2tog) 6 times (6 sts).
Fasten off. Leave a yarn tail to sew to the mini cactus.

MINI CACTUS

Using 3.5mm hook and A, make a magic ring.

Round 1: 1 ch, 6 dc into centre of the ring.
Round 2: 2 dc into each st (12 sts).
Rounds 3–6: Work 4 rounds straight.
Stuff with a small amount of stuffing.
Round 7: (dc2tog) 6 times (6 sts).
Fasten off. Leave a yarn tail to sew to the small cactus.

SOIL

Using 3.5mm hook and C, make a magic ring.

Round 1: 1 ch, 6 dc into centre of the ring.
Round 2: 2 dc into each st (12 sts).
Round 3: (1 dc, dc2inc) 6 times (18 sts).
Rounds 4–7: Work 4 rounds straight.
Round 8: (1 dc, dc2tog) 6 times (12 sts).
Stuff with a small amount of stuffing.
Round 9: (Dc2tog) 6 times (6 sts).
Fasten off. Leave a yarn tail to sew to the base of the small cactus.

MAKING UP

Using a small amount of pink yarn, sew a tiny mouth between the eyes on the small cactus.

Use a long strand of B to create segments on the small cactus. Bring your tapestry needle up through the base to the top of the cactus. Pull the yarn around the outside of the cactus. Repeat four times.

Sew the mini cactus to the top of the small cactus. Sew firmly to the top of the soil. Place into a small pot (see pages 124–5).

MEXICAN BALL CACTUS

This jolly fellow will brighten every home. His ribbed effect is created with the front and back post technique. You can change the colour of the flower to suit your cactus style.

YOU WILL NEED

- Scheepjes Catona, 100% cotton (136yd/125m per 50g ball): 1 x 50g ball in 515 Emerald (A)
- Scheepjes Catona, 100% cotton (27yd/25m per 10g ball): 1 x 10g ball in 281 Tangerine (B) and 522 Primrose (C)
- Stylecraft Special DK, 100% acrylic (323yd/295m per 100g ball): A small amount of 1054 Walnut (D)
- 3mm (UK 11:US –) crochet hook
- 3.5mm (UK 9:US E/4) crochet hook
- Tapestry needle, stitch marker, safety pin, small fork
- Small bag of rice or lentils
- Polyester stuffing
- A strand of black yarn
- 2 x ⅜in (10mm) black safety eyes

FINISHED SIZE

The cactus is about 3½in (9cm) tall.

TECHNIQUES

Magic ring
Chain (ch)
Slip stitch (sl st)
Double crochet (dc)
dc2inc
dc2tog
Treble crochet (tr)
Raised treble front (Rtrf)
Raised treble back (Rtrb)

NOTE

The cactus is worked in spirals using raised (post) front and back stitches (see page 119). Place a marker at the beginning of each round so you know where you are in the pattern.

CACTUS

Using 3.5mm hook and A, make a magic ring.
Round 1: 1 ch, 6 dc into the centre of the ring.
Round 2: 2 dc into each st (12 sts).
Round 3: (1 dc, dc2inc) 6 times (18 sts).
Round 4: (Tr2inc) 18 times (36 sts).
Rounds 5–13: (1 Rtrf, 1 Rtrb) 18 times (36 sts).
Round 14: (Dc2tog) 18 times (18 sts).
Stop at this point, put a safety pin onto the loop on the hook. Using the photograph as a guide, place safety eyes and sew a mouth onto the fabric of the crochet. Place loop back on hook.
Round 15: (1 dc, dc2tog) 6 times (12 sts).
Round 16: (Dc2tog) 6 times (6 sts).
Fasten off and weave in ends.

FLOWER

Using 3mm hook and B, make a magic ring.
Round 1: 1 ch, 5 dc into the centre of the ring, join with a sl st.
Round 2: * 6 ch, 5 sl st down ch, sl st in same st, 6 ch, 5 sl st down ch, sl st in next st; rep from * 5 times (10 petals).
Fasten off and leave a tail of yarn.

FLOWER CENTRE

Using C, wrap a fork with yarn approximately 8 times halfway down the fork to make a thin pompom (see page 123). Secure with a 4in (10cm) strand of C in the centre and cut the sides of the wrapped yarn. Press the pompom flat.

SOIL

Using 3.5mm hook and D, make a magic ring.
Round 1: 1 ch, 6 dc into the centre of the ring.
Round 2: 2 dc into each st (12 sts).
Round 3: (1 dc, dc2inc) 6 times (18 sts).
Round 4: (2 dc, dc2inc) 6 times (24 sts).
Round 5: (3 dc, dc2inc) 6 times (30 sts).
Round 6: (4 dc, dc2inc) 6 times (36 sts).
Rounds 7–11: Work 5 rounds straight.
Round 12: (4 dc, dc2tog) 6 times (30 sts).
Round 13: (3 dc, dc2tog) 6 times (24 sts).
Round 14: (2 dc, dc2tog) 6 times (18 sts).
Place a small bag of rice or lentils in the base and then stuff firmly with polyester stuffing.
Round 15: (1 dc, dc2tog) 6 times (12 sts).
Round 16: (Dc2tog) 6 times (6 sts).
Using a tapestry needle, weave this yarn through the last dc sts of the round and gather hole together. Fasten off and weave in ends.

MAKING UP

Sew the flower centre to the middle of the flower. Sew the flower securely to the top of the cactus. Sew the base of the cactus securely to the top of the soil.

Place into a small pot (see pages 124–5).

PERKY POINSETTIA

This beautiful and festive plant brightens even the dullest winter days, but outside their tropical home, it is hard to keep them alive. Not this glamour puss: this cute version will be forever in bloom on your mantelpiece.

NOTE

This flower is made by sewing five petals together and then sewing the flower face to the middle of the petals.

YOU WILL NEED

- **Drops Nord 4ply, 45% alpaca, 30% polyamide, 25% wool (186yd/170m per 50g ball): 1 x 50g ball in 14 Red (A) and 19 Forest Green (B)**
- **Stylecraft Special DK, 100% acrylic (323yd/295m per 100g ball): A small amount of 1054 Walnut (C)**
- **3mm (UK 11:US –) crochet hook**
- **3.5mm (UK 9:US E/4) crochet hook**
- **Tapestry needle and safety pin**
- **Small bag of rice or lentils**
- **Polyester stuffing**
- **A strand of black and a strand of yellow yarn**
- **2 x ⅛in (4mm) black safety eyes**
- **Chenille wire**
- **Floristry wire**

FINISHED SIZE

The flower head is approximately 5¼in (13cm) wide.

TECHNIQUES

Magic ring
Chain (ch)
Slip stitch (sl st)
Double crochet (dc)
dc2inc
dc2tog
Double treble (dtr)

PETALS (MAKE 5)

Using 3mm hook and A, make a magic ring.
Round 1: 1 ch, 4 dc into the centre of the ring.
Round 2: (Dc2inc) 4 times (8 sts).
Round 3: (3 dc, dc2inc) twice (10 sts).
Round 4: (4 dc, dc2inc) twice (12 sts).
Round 5: (5 dc, dc2inc) twice (14 sts).
Round 6: (6 dc, dc2inc) twice (16 sts).
Round 7: (7 dc, dc2inc) twice (18 sts).
Rounds 8–13: Work 6 rounds straight.
Round 14: (1 dc, dc2tog) 6 times (12 sts).
Round 15: (Dc2tog) 6 times (6 sts).
Fasten off and leave a tail of yarn.

FLOWER FACE

Using 3mm hook and A, make a magic ring.
Round 1: 1 ch, 6 dc into the centre of the ring, join with a sl st.
Round 2: (Dc2inc) 6 times (12 sts).
Round 3: (1 dc, dc2inc) 6 times (18 sts).
Round 4: Work 1 round straight (18 sts).
Round 5: (1 dc, dc2tog) 6 times (12 sts).
Remove the loop from the hook and place onto a safety pin. Using the photograph as a guide, position the safety eyes. Use a strand of black yarn to embroider the mouth. Use a strand of yellow yarn to sew a few running stitches around the edge of the face. Fasten off and leave a tail of yarn.

FLOWER BACK

Using 3mm hook and B, make a magic ring.
Round 1: Ch 1, 6 dc into the centre of the ring, join with a sl st.
Round 2: (Dc2inc) 6 times(12 sts).
Round 3: (1 dc, dc2inc) 6 times (18 sts).
Fasten off and leave a tail of yarn.

STEM

Using 3mm hook and B, ch 4 sts, sl st in first ch to create a loop.
Round 1: 1 ch, 4 dc into the centre of the loop.
Rounds 2–16: Work 15 rounds straight (4 sts).
Fasten off and leave a tail of yarn.

LEAF (MAKE 2)

Using 3mm hook and B, make a magic ring.

Round 1: 1 ch, 4 dc into the centre of the ring.

Round 2: (Dc2inc) 4 times (8 sts).

Round 3: (3 dc, dc2inc) twice (10 sts).

Round 4: (4 dc, dc2inc) twice (12 sts).

Round 5: (5 dc, dc2inc) twice (14 sts).

Rounds 6–14: Work 9 rounds straight.

Round 15: (5 dc, dc2tog) twice (12 sts).

Rounds 16–17: Work 2 rounds straight.

Round 18: (Dc2tog) 6 times (6 sts).

Fasten off and leave a tail of yarn.

SOIL

Using 3.5mm hook and C, make a magic ring.

Round 1: 1 ch, 6 dc into the centre of the ring.

Round 2: 2 dc into each st (12 sts).

Round 3: (1 dc, dc2inc) 6 times (18 sts).

Round 4: (2 dc, dc2inc) 6 times (24 sts).

Round 5: (3 dc, dc2inc) 6 times (30 sts).

Round 6: (4 dc, dc2inc) 6 times (36 sts).

Rounds 7–11: Work 5 rounds straight.

Round 12: (4 dc, dc2tog) 6 times (30 sts).

Round 13: (3 dc, dc2tog) 6 times (24 sts).

Round 14: (2 dc, dc2tog) 6 times (18 sts).

Place a small bag of rice or lentils in the base and then stuff firmly with polyester stuffing.

Round 15: (1 dc, dc2tog) 6 times (12 sts).

Round 16: (Dc2tog) 6 times (6 sts).

Using a tapestry needle, weave this yarn through the last dc sts of the round and gather hole together. Fasten off and weave in ends.

MAKING UP

Fold each petal in half and press it flat with your hand. Arrange the five petals to form a star and, using the tail of yarn, sew the end rows together to form a flat star. Sew the flower face to the middle of the petals.

Fold a chenille wire in half and feed this through the middle of the flower stem. Position the stem so that it meets the centre back of the flower. Place the flower back over the top of the stem. Use the yarn tail to whip stitch (see page 122) the flower back to the stitches at the base of the petals. Poke the stem into the centre of the soil.

Place a piece of floristry wire in the leaf so that you can bend and position the leaf to suit your arrangement. Sew the base of the leaves ¾in (2cm) from the bottom of the stem. With a few small stitches, sew the base of the stem to the top of the soil. Place into a small pot (see pages 124–5).

MINI MONSTERA

The ultimate house plant, this time not monstrous but in a cheery mini form. I have used some little flat buttons for eyes. Put a face on just one leaf or create a different character on each one.

YOU WILL NEED

- **Drops Alpaca 4ply, 100% alpaca (183yd/167m per 50g ball): 1 x 50g ball in 7815 Forest Mix (A)**
- **Stylecraft Special DK, 100% acrylic (323yd/295m per 100g ball): A small amount of 1054 Walnut (B)**
- **3mm (UK 11:US –) crochet hook**
- **3.5mm (UK 9:US E/4) crochet hook**
- **Tapestry needle and stitch marker**
- **Small bag of rice or lentils**
- **Polyester stuffing**
- **A strand of black yarn**
- **Ricorumi 4 x 3/16in (5mm) black button eyes**
- **Chenille wire**

NOTE

The leaves are created by working in the round and then sewing in the gaps created in the work to create the slashes in the leaves. This is one pattern that requires you to have a marker at the beginning of each round and it is worth reading your pattern through before you start.

FINISHED SIZE

The large leaves are approximately 5in (12cm) tall and 4in (10cm) wide. The smaller leaf is approximately 3¾in (9.5cm) tall and 3¾in (9.5cm) wide.

TECHNIQUES

Magic ring	dc2inc
Chain (ch)	dc2tog
Slip stitch (sl st)	Double treble (dtr)
Double crochet (dc)	

LARGE LEAF (MAKE 2)

Using 3.5mm hook and A, make a magic ring.
Round 1: 1 ch, 6 dc into the centre of the ring.
Round 2: 2 dc into each st (12 sts).
Round 3: (1 dc, dc2inc) 6 times (18 sts).
Round 4: (8 dc, dc2inc) twice (20 sts).
Fasten off the first top.
Make a second, but do not fasten off.
Round 5: Work 20 sts around the first top and then 20 sts around the second, joining both together (40 sts).
Rounds 6–7: Work 2 rounds straight.
Round 8: 9 dc, dc2inc, 19 dc, dc2inc, 10 dc (42 sts).
Rounds 9–11: Work 3 rounds straight.
Round 12: 9 dc, dc2tog, 20 dc, dc2tog, 9 dc (40 sts).
Slash Round 13: 5 dc, 9 ch, miss 10 dc, 15 dc, dc2tog, 8 dc (38 sts).
Round 14: Work 1 dc into each st and ch st (38 sts).
Round 15: Work 1 round straight (38 sts).
Slash Round 16: 8 dc, dc2tog, 12 dc, dc2tog, 11 ch, miss 12 dc, 2 dc (36 sts).
Round 17: Work 1 dc into each st and ch st (36 sts).
Slash Round 18: 5 dc, 9 ch, miss 10 dc, 11 dc, dc2tog, 8 dc (34 sts).
Round 19: Work 1 dc into each st and ch st (34 sts).
Round 20: 9 dc, dc2tog, 15 dc, dc2tog, 6 dc (32 sts).
Round 21: 8 dc, dc2tog, 14 dc, dc2tog, 6 dc (30 sts).
Round 22: (4 dc, dc2tog) 5 times (25 sts).
Round 23: (3 dc, dc2tog) 5 times (20 sts).
Round 24: (2 dc, dc2tog) 5 times (15 sts).
Round 25: (1 dc, dc2tog) 5 times (10 sts).
Rounds 26–27: Work 2 rounds straight.
Round 28: (Dc2tog) 5 times (5 sts).
Fasten off and weave in ends.

SMALL LEAF

Using 3.5mm hook and A, make a magic ring.

Round 1: 1 ch, 6 dc into the centre of the ring.

Round 2: 2 dc into each st (12 sts).

Round 3: (1 dc, dc2inc) 6 times (18 sts).

Round 4: (8 dc, dc2inc) twice (20 sts).

Fasten off the first top.

Make a second, but do not fasten off.

Round 5: Work 20 sts around the first top and then 20 sts around the second, joining both together (40 sts).

Rounds 6–9: Work 4 rounds straight.

Round 10: 9 dc, dc2tog, 18 dc, dc2tog, 9 dc (38 sts).

Round 11: Work 1 round straight (38 sts).

Round 12: 9 dc, dc2tog, 17 dc, dc2tog, 8 dc (36 sts).

Round 13: Work 1 round straight (36 sts).

Round 14: 8 dc, dc2tog, 16 dc, dc2tog, 8 dc (34 sts).

Round 15: Work 1 round straight (34 sts).

Round 16: 7 dc, dc2tog, 15 dc, dc2tog, 8 dc (32 sts).

Round 17: 7 dc, dc2tog, 14 dc, dc2tog, 7 dc (30 sts).

Round 18: (4 dc, dc2tog) 5 times (25 sts).

Round 19: (3 dc, dc2tog) 5 times (20 sts).

Round 20: (2 dc, dc2tog) 5 times (15 sts).

Round 21: (1 dc, dc2tog) 5 times (10 sts).

Rounds 22–23: Work 2 rounds straight.

Round 24: (Dc2tog) 5 times (5 sts).

Fasten off and weave in ends.

LONG STEM

Using 3mm hook and A, ch 4 sts, sl st in first ch to create a loop.

Round 1: Ch 1, 4 dc into the centre of the loop.

Rounds 2–25: Work 24 rounds straight. (4 sts).

Fasten off and leave a tail of yarn.

SHORT STEM (MAKE 2)

Using 3mm hook and A, ch 4 sts, sl st in first ch to create a loop.

Round 1: Ch 1, 4 dc into the centre of the loop.

Rounds 2–20: Work 19 rounds straight. (4 sts).

Fasten off and leave a tail of yarn.

SOIL

Using 3.5mm hook and B, make a magic ring.
Round 1: 1 ch, 6 dc into the centre of the ring.
Round 2: 2 dc into each st (12 sts).
Round 3: (1 dc, dc2inc) 6 times (18 sts).
Round 4: (2 dc, dc2inc) 6 times (24 sts).
Round 5: (3 dc, dc2inc) 6 times (30 sts).
Round 6: (4 dc, dc2inc) 6 times (36 sts).
Round 7: (5 dc, dc2inc) 6 times (42 sts).
Rounds 8–15: Work 8 rounds straight.
Round 16: (5 dc, dc2tog) 6 times (36 sts).
Round 17: (4 dc, dc2tog) 6 times (30 sts).
Round 18: (3 dc, dc2tog) 6 times (24 sts).
Round 19: (2 dc, dc2tog) 6 times (18 sts).
Place a small bag of rice or lentils in the base and then stuff firmly with polyester stuffing.
Round 20: (1 dc, dc2tog) 6 times (12 sts).
Round 21: (Dc2tog) 6 times (6 sts).
Using a tapestry needle, weave this yarn through the last dc sts of the round and gather hole together. Fasten off and weave in ends.

MAKING UP

Fold each leaf in half and press it flat with your hand. Arrange so that the leaf looks like a heart with the top having two curved edges. Use strands of A to sew the edges of the slashed rows together. Using the photograph as a guide, place the plastic eyes and stitch the mouth on the face using black yarn.

Fold a chenille wire in half and then feed this through the middle of each stem. Bend the top of the stem over slightly. Position the stem so that it meets the centre top of the leaf. Use a strand of A to whip stitch (see page 122) the stem to the back of the leaf. Poke the stem into the centre of the soil. With a few small stitches, sew the three stems together near the base. With a few small stitches, sew the base of the stems to the top of the soil. Place into a small pot (see pages 124–5).

CURLY WURLY PLANT

What a very satisfying project this is to make. Once you have made one, you won't want to stop! For extra realism, try using a variegated yarn.

YOU WILL NEED

- **Rico Ricorumi Spin Spin DK, 100% Cotton (126yd/115m per 50g ball): 1 x 50g ball in 013 Green (A)**
- **Stylecraft Special DK, 100% acrylic (323yd/295m per 100g ball): 1 x 100g ball in 1001 White (B) and 1054 Walnut (C)**
- **3.5mm (UK 9:US E/4) crochet hook**
- **Tapestry needle**
- **Polyester stuffing**
- **2 x ⅜in (10mm) black safety eyes**
- **A strand of black yarn and one of pink**
- **A small piece of cardboard**

FINISHED SIZE

The longest spiral is approximately 5in (12.5cm) long.

TECHNIQUES

Magic ring
Chain (ch)
Slip stitch (sl st)
Double crochet (dc)
dc2inc
dc2tog
Back loop only (blo)

NOTE

The spirals are worked separately and then sewn together when assembled at the end. The crochet will naturally spiral, but to get an even look, twist the length of the spiral around your fingers.

LARGE SPIRAL

Row 1: Using 3.5mm hook and A, 34 ch.
Row 2: 1 tr in 4th ch from hook, 4 tr into each ch to end.
Fasten off and leave a long tail of yarn.

MEDIUM SPIRAL (MAKE 4)

Row 1: Using 3.5mm hook and A, 24 ch.
Row 2: 1 tr in 4th ch from hook, 4 tr into each ch to end.
Fasten off and leave a long tail of yarn.

SMALL SPIRAL (MAKE 3)

Row 1: Using 3.5mm hook and A, 14 ch.
Row 2: 1 tr in 4th ch from hook, 4 tr into each ch to end.
Fasten off and leave a long tail of yarn.

POT

Using 3.5mm hook and B, make a magic ring.

Round 1: 1 ch, 8 dc into the centre of the ring.
Round 2: 2 dc into each st (16 sts).
Round 3: (1 dc, dc2inc) 8 times (24 sts).
Round 4: (2 dc, dc2inc) 8 times (32 sts).
Round 5: Work 1 round (32 sts).
Round 6: Work 1 round blo (32 sts).
Round 7: (3 dc, dc2inc) 8 times (40 sts).
Round 8: Work 1 round (40 sts).
Round 9: (4 dc, dc2inc) 8 times (48 sts).
Round 10: Work 1 round (48 sts).
Round 11: (5 dc, dc2inc) 8 times (56 sts).
Rounds 12–16: Work 5 rounds straight.
Round 17: (5 dc, dc2tog) 8 times (48 sts).
Round 18: Work 1 round (48 sts).
Round 19: (4 dc, dc2tog) 8 times (40 sts).
Round 20: Work 1 round (40 sts).
Round 21: (3 dc, dc2tog) 8 times (32 sts).
Round 22: Work 1 round blo (32 sts).
Fasten off and weave in ends.

SOIL

Using 3.5mm hook and C, make a magic ring.

Round 1: 1 ch, 6 dc into the centre of the ring.
Round 2: 2 dc into each st (12 sts).
Round 3: (1 dc, dc2inc) 6 times (18 sts).
Round 4: (2 dc, dc2inc) 6 times (24 sts).
Round 5: (3 dc, dc2inc) 6 times (30 sts).
Round 6: (4 dc, dc2inc) 6 times (36 sts).
Rounds 7–13: Work 7 rounds straight.
Round 14: (4 dc, dc2tog) 6 times (30 sts).
Round 15: (3 dc, dc2tog) 6 times (24 sts).
Round 16: (2 dc, dc2tog) 6 times (18 sts).
Stuff firmly with polyester stuffing.
Round 17: (1 dc, dc2tog) 6 times (12 sts).
Round 18: (Dc2tog) 6 times (6 sts).
Using a tapestry needle, weave this yarn through the last dc sts of the round and gather hole together. Fasten off and weave in ends.

MAKING UP

Evenly sew the spirals together at the ends. Sew the attached spirals firmly to the centre of the soil. Space out and arrange the spirals so they fall naturally over the edge of the pot.

Using the photograph as a guide, place the plastic eyes and stitch the mouth using black yarn. Sew a star of pink stitches on each side of the face to create rosy cheeks.

Place a small piece of cardboard (about 2¼in/6cm in diameter) in the base of the pot. Put a little bit of stuffing in the base of the pot. Pop the plant with its soil into the pot and arrange the spirals to look like hair.

STRING OF PEARLS

This trailing plant makes a brilliant addition to your collection and uses bobble stitches to create its pea-sized leaves on long, trailing stems. It's ideal for displaying on a shelf or in a hanging pot holder.

YOU WILL NEED

- Scheepjes Softfun, 60% cotton, 40% acrylic (153yd/140m per 50g ball): 1 x 50g ball in 2531 Olive (A), 2533 Wheat (B) and 2623 Chocolate (C)
- 3.5mm (UK 9:US E/4) crochet hook
- Tapestry needle
- Polyester stuffing
- A small piece of cardboard
- 2 x 3/8in (10mm) black safety eyes
- A strand of black yarn

FINISHED SIZE

The plant in its pot is approximately 3½in (9cm) tall and 3½in (9cm) wide. The longest strands are approximately 7in (18cm) long.

TECHNIQUES

Magic ring
Chain (ch)
Slip stitch (sl st)
Double crochet (dc)
dc2inc
Half treble (htr)
Back loop only (blo)
Bobble

NOTE

You can make bobble stitches with any of the standard stitches and as large or small as you like. If you want to create longer strands, simply repeat the bobble count more. For instructions, see page 115.

LARGE STRAND (MAKE 4)

Using 3.5mm hook and A:

Row 1: 3 ch, 3 htr bobble in first ch, *5 ch, 3 htr bobble in 3rd ch from hook; rep from * 5 times, 5 ch (7 bobbles). Fasten off and leave a tail of yarn.

SMALL STRAND (MAKE 3)

Using 3.5mm hook and A:

Row 1: 3 ch, 3 htr bobble in first ch, *7 ch, 3 htr bobble in 3rd ch from hook; rep from * twice, 5 ch (4 bobbles). Fasten off and leave a tail of yarn.

POT

Using 3.5mm hook and B, make a magic ring.

Round 1: 1 ch, 8 dc into the centre of the ring.
Round 2: 2 dc into each st (16 sts).
Round 3: (1 dc, dc2inc) 8 times (24 sts).
Round 4: (2 dc, dc2inc) 8 times (32 sts).
Round 5: Work 1 round (32 sts).
Round 6: Work 1 round blo (32 sts).
Rounds 7–9: Work 3 rounds straight.
Round 10: (3 dc, dc2inc) 8 times (40 sts).
Rounds 11–12: Work 2 rounds straight.
Round 13: (4 dc, dc2inc) 8 times (48 sts).
Rounds 14–18: Work 5 rounds straight.
Rounds 19–20: Work 2 rounds blo (48 sts).
Round 21: 1 htr blo in each st (48 sts).
Round 22: Work 1 round blo (48 sts).
Fasten off and weave in ends.

SOIL TOP

Using 3.5mm hook and C, make a magic ring.

Round 1: Ch 1, 8 dc into the centre of the ring, join with a sl st.
Round 2: (Dc2inc) 8 times (16 sts).
Round 3: (1 dc, dc2inc) 8 times (24 sts).
Round 4: (2 dc, dc2inc) 8 times (32 sts).
Round 5: (3 dc, dc2inc) 8 times (40 sts).
Round 6: (4 dc, dc2inc) 8 times (48 sts).
Round 7: Work 1 round straight.
Fasten off and leave a long tail of yarn.

MAKING UP

Using the photograph as a guide, place the plastic eyes and stitch the mouth using black yarn. Place a small piece of cardboard (around 2¼in/6cm in diameter) in the base of the pot. Firmly stuff the pot. Fold the last two rounds of the pot over. Place the soil top on top and whip stitch (see page 122) the last rounds of the pot and the soil together.

Using the long tail of yarn, sew each end of the strands to the centre of the soil and drape the long strings over the edge of the pot.

SWEETHEART PLANT

Who wouldn't want to give this cuddly version of a popular succulent to a loved one? Sneak it onto a desk, and you have the perfect Valentine's gift!

NOTE

This plant is worked in spirals using the standard amigurumi technique. You will make one side of the top of the heart and then make a second. Without fastening off, you then crochet both together to form the heart.

YOU WILL NEED

- **Stylecraft Special DK, 100% acrylic (323yd/295m per 100g ball):**
  A small amount of 1009 Bottle (A) and 1054 Walnut (B)
- **3.5mm (UK 9:US E/4) crochet hook**
- **Tapestry needle**
- **Polyester stuffing**
- **2 x ⅜in (10mm) black safety eyes**
- **A small piece of white felt**
- **A strand of pink yarn**

FINISHED SIZE

The cactus is approximately 3½in (9cm) tall.

TECHNIQUES

Magic ring
Chain (ch)
Slip stitch (sl st)
Double crochet (dc)
dc2inc
dc2tog

LEAF

Using 3.5mm hook and A, make a magic ring.

Make 2 tops:

Round 1: 1 ch, 6 dc into the centre of the ring.

Round 2: 2 dc into each st (12 sts).

Round 3: (1 dc, dc2inc) 6 times (18 sts).

Round 4: (8 dc, dc2inc) twice (20 sts).

Fasten off the first top.

Make a second, but do not fasten off.

Round 5: Work 20 sts around the first top and then 20 sts around the second, joining both together (40 sts).

Rounds 6–8: Work 3 rounds straight.

Round 9: 9 dc, dc2tog, 18 dc, dc2tog, 9 dc (38 sts).

Round 10–11: Work 2 rounds straight.

Round 12: 9 dc, dc2tog, 17 dc, dc2tog, 8 dc (36 sts).

Round 13: Work 1 round straight (36 sts).

Round 14: 9 dc, dc2tog, 16 dc, dc2tog, 7 dc (34 sts).

Round 15: Work 1 round straight (34 sts).

Round 16: 9 dc, dc2tog, 15 dc, dc2tog, 6 dc (32 sts).

Round 17: Work 1 round straight (32 sts).

Fasten off. Leave a yarn tail to sew to the soil.

SOIL

Using 3.5mm hook and B, make a magic ring.

Round 1: 1 ch, 6 dc into the centre of the ring.

Round 2: 2 dc into each st (12 sts).

Round 3: (1 dc, dc2inc) 6 times (18 sts).

Round 4: (2 dc, dc2inc) 6 times (24 sts).

Round 5: (3 dc, dc2inc) 6 times (30 sts).

Round 6: (4 dc, dc2inc) 6 times (36 sts).

Rounds 7–12: Work 6 rounds straight.

Round 13: (4 dc, dc2tog) 6 times (30 sts).

Round 14: (3 dc, dc2tog) 6 times (24 sts).

Round 15: (2 dc, dc2tog) 6 times (18 sts).

Stuff firmly with polyester stuffing.

Round 16: (1 dc, dc2tog) 6 times (12 sts).

Round 17: (Dc2tog) 6 times (6 sts).

Using a tapestry needle, weave this yarn through the last dc sts of the round and gather hole together. Fasten off and weave in ends.

MAKING UP

Take two small pieces of white felt. Make a small hole in the centre of each piece and poke the shank of the safety eye through the centre. Using small scissors, trim the felt so that it is just a little larger than the black plastic circle of the eye. Then, using the photograph as a guide, position and secure the safety eyes on the leaf.

Stitch the mouth using the pink yarn. Stuff the leaf firmly making sure there is enough stuffing in the top of the heart. Using the tails of yarn, sew firmly to the soil. Place into a small pot (see pages 124–5).

SNAKE'S TONGUE PLANT

This plant is so striking and distinctive. In real life, the edges of its long leaves are spiky, but this cheerful fellow is perfectly soft to the touch.

YOU WILL NEED

- **Stylecraft Special DK, 100% acrylic (323yd/295m per 100g ball): 1 x 100g ball in 1009 Bottle (A), 1823 Mustard (B), 1064 Mocha (C) and 1054 Walnut (D)**
- **Rowan Kidsilk Haze, 70% mohair, 30% silk (230yd/210m per 25g ball): 1 x 25g ball in 721 Olive (E) and 684 Eve Green (F)**
- **3.5mm (UK 9:US E/4) crochet hook**
- **Tapestry needle**
- **Polyester stuffing**
- **A small piece of cardboard**
- **2 x ⅜in (10mm) black safety eyes**
- **A strand of black yarn**

FINISHED SIZE

The plant and pot are approximately 8in (20cm) tall and 3½in (9cm) in diameter.

TECHNIQUES

Magic ring
Chain (ch)
Slip stitch (sl st)
Double crochet (dc)
dc2inc
Half treble crochet (htr)
Back loop only (blo)
Crab stitch

NOTE

The plant is made of individual leaves which you position on a circle of brown soil. The leaves are worked in rows and then each leaf is edged with a crab stitch. Each leaf and edging is worked holding two yarns together. They are then sewn on the top of the pot.

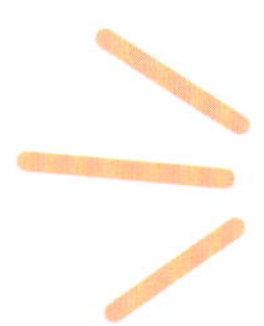

LEAF (MAKE 7)

Row 1: Using 3.5mm hook and holding A and E together, 2 ch.
Row 2: 3 dc in 2nd ch from hook, turn (3 sts).
Rows 3: 1 ch, 1 dc in each st to end, turn (3 sts).
Row 4: 1 ch, dc2inc, 1 dc, dc2inc, turn (5 sts).
Rows 5: 1 ch, 1 dc in each st to end, turn (5 sts).
Row 6: 1 ch, dc2inc, 3 dc, dc2inc, turn (7 sts).
Rows 7–18: Work 12 rows straight. Fasten off A and E.
Edging:
Next row: Join in B and F together, 1 ch, starting at row 18, crab stitch around the row ends on both sides of the leaf ending back at row 18.
Fasten off and weave in all ends.

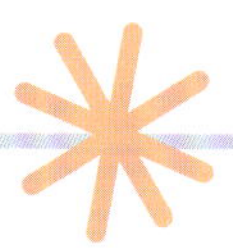

POT

Using 3.5mm hook and C, make a magic ring.

Round 1: 1 ch, 8 dc into the centre of the ring.
Round 2: 2 dc into each st (16 sts).
Round 3: (1 dc, dc2inc) 8 times (24 sts).
Round 4: (2 dc, dc2inc) 8 times (32 sts).
Round 5: Work 1 round (32 sts).
Round 6: Work 1 round blo (32 sts).
Rounds 7–9: Work 3 rounds straight.
Round 10: (3 dc, dc2inc) 8 times (40 sts).
Rounds 11–12: Work 2 rounds straight.
Round 13: (4 dc, dc2inc) 8 times (48 sts).
Rounds 14–18: Work 5 rounds straight.
Rounds 19–20: Work 2 rounds blo (48 sts).
Round 21: 1 htr blo in each st (48 sts).
Round 22: Work 1 round blo (48 sts).
Fasten off and weave in ends.

SOIL TOP

Using 3.5mm hook and D, make a magic ring.

Round 1: 1 ch, 8 dc into the centre of the ring, join with a sl st.
Round 2: (Dc2inc) 8 times (16 sts).
Round 3: (1 dc, dc2inc) 8 times (24 sts).
Round 4: (2 dc, dc2inc) 8 times (32 sts).
Round 5: (3 dc, dc2inc) 8 times (40 sts).
Round 6: (4 dc, dc2inc) 8 times (48 sts).
Round 7: Work 1 round straight.
Fasten off and leave a long tail of yarn.

MAKING UP

Using the photograph as a guide, place the plastic eyes and stitch the mouth using black yarn.

Place a small piece of cardboard (around 2¼in/6cm in diameter) in the base of the pot. Firmly stuff the pot. Fold the last two rounds of the pot over. Place the soil top on top and whip stitch (see page 122) the last rounds of the pot and the soil together.

Overlap the edges of three leaves to form the centre and then overlap the edge of each flowing leaf. Sew each leaf at the base to secure the edge. Sew the base of the plant to the centre of the soil.

SOFT CHRISTMAS WREATH

This not-so-spiky holly wreath is a cuddly friend to brighten the festive season. Wouldn't this make a great gift on top of a stocking?

YOU WILL NEED

- **Stylecraft Squeeze Me DK, 100% polyester (219yd/200m per 100g ball): 1 x 100g ball in 5610 Emerald Green (A), a small amount of 5614 Apple Green (B)**
- **Scheepjes Catona, 100% cotton (27yd/25m per 10g ball): 1 x 10g ball in 115 Hot Red (C)**
- **3.5mm (UK 9:US E/4) crochet hook**
- **Polyester stuffing**
- **Tapestry needle and stitch marker**
- **A pair of ⅜in (10mm) safety eyes**
- **A strand of black yarn**

FINISHED SIZE

The wreath is approximately 6in (15cm) in diameter.

TECHNIQUES

Magic ring
Chain (ch)
Slip stitch (sl st)
Cross double crochet (x-dc)
dc2inc
dc2tog

NOTE

The wreath base is made like a circular doughnut. You start in the centre and increase to create the larger circle and then decrease again to the centre. The pattern uses the cross double crochet technique (see page 110). Place a marker at the beginning of each round so you know where you are in the pattern. The holly leaves, mistletoe and berries are made separately and sewn on at the end.

WREATH BASE

Using 3.5mm hook and A, 24 ch, join with a sl st to make a ring.
Round 1: (2 x-dc, x-dc2inc) 8 times (32 sts).
Round 2: (3 x-dc, x-dc2inc) 8 times (40 sts).
Round 3: (X-dc2inc, 4 x-dc) 8 times (48 sts).
Round 4: (5 x-dc, x-dc2inc) 8 times (56 sts).
Round 5: 3 x-dc, x-dc2inc, (6 x-dc, x-dc2inc) 7 times, 3 x-dc (64 sts).
Rounds 6–13: Work 8 rounds straight.
Round 14: 3 x-dc, x-dc2tog (6 x-dc, x-dc2tog) 7 times, 3 x-dc (56 sts).
Round 15: (5 x-dc, x-dc2tog) 8 times (48 sts).
Round 16: (X-dc2tog, 4 x-dc) 8 times (40 sts).
Round 17: (3 x-dc, x-dc2tog) 8 times (32 sts).
Round 18: (2 x-dc, x-dc2tog) 8 times (24 sts).
Round 19: Work 1 round straight.

Fasten off and leave a 12in (30cm) tail of yarn. Sew the first and last round together to form a ring. Leave a small hole. Using the photograph as a guide, position the eyes and sew on the mouth. Stuff the ring firmly. Sew the final stitches of the inner ring together. Weave in ends.

HOLLY LEAF (MAKE 12)

Using 3.5mm hook and A, 6 ch.

Row 1: 1 x-dc in 2nd ch from hook, (1 tr, 2 ch, 1 tr) in next ch, 1 x-dc in next ch, (1 x-dc, 1 tr, 2 ch, 1 tr, 1 x-dc) in next ch, sl st in last ch, (now turn and work down the other side of the foundation ch), (1 x-dc, 1 tr, 2 ch, 1 tr, 1 x-dc) in next ch, 1 x-dc in next ch, (1 tr, 2 ch, 1 tr) in next ch, 1 x-dc in next ch, sl st to join. Fasten off and leave a tail of yarn.

MISTLETOE (MAKE 9)

Using 3.5mm hook and B, 12 ch.

Row 1: 1 x-dc in 2nd ch from hook, 1 htr, 1 tr, 1 htr, 1 x-dc, 1 sl st, 1 x-dc, 1 htr, 1 tr, 1 htr, 1 sl st in last ch.

Fasten off and leave a tail of yarn. Row 1 forms the two leaves of the mistletoe.

BERRY (MAKE 4)

Using 3.5mm hook and C, make a magic ring.

Round 1: 2 ch, 46 tr into the centre of the ring. Sl st into 2nd chain.

Fasten off and leave a tail of yarn.

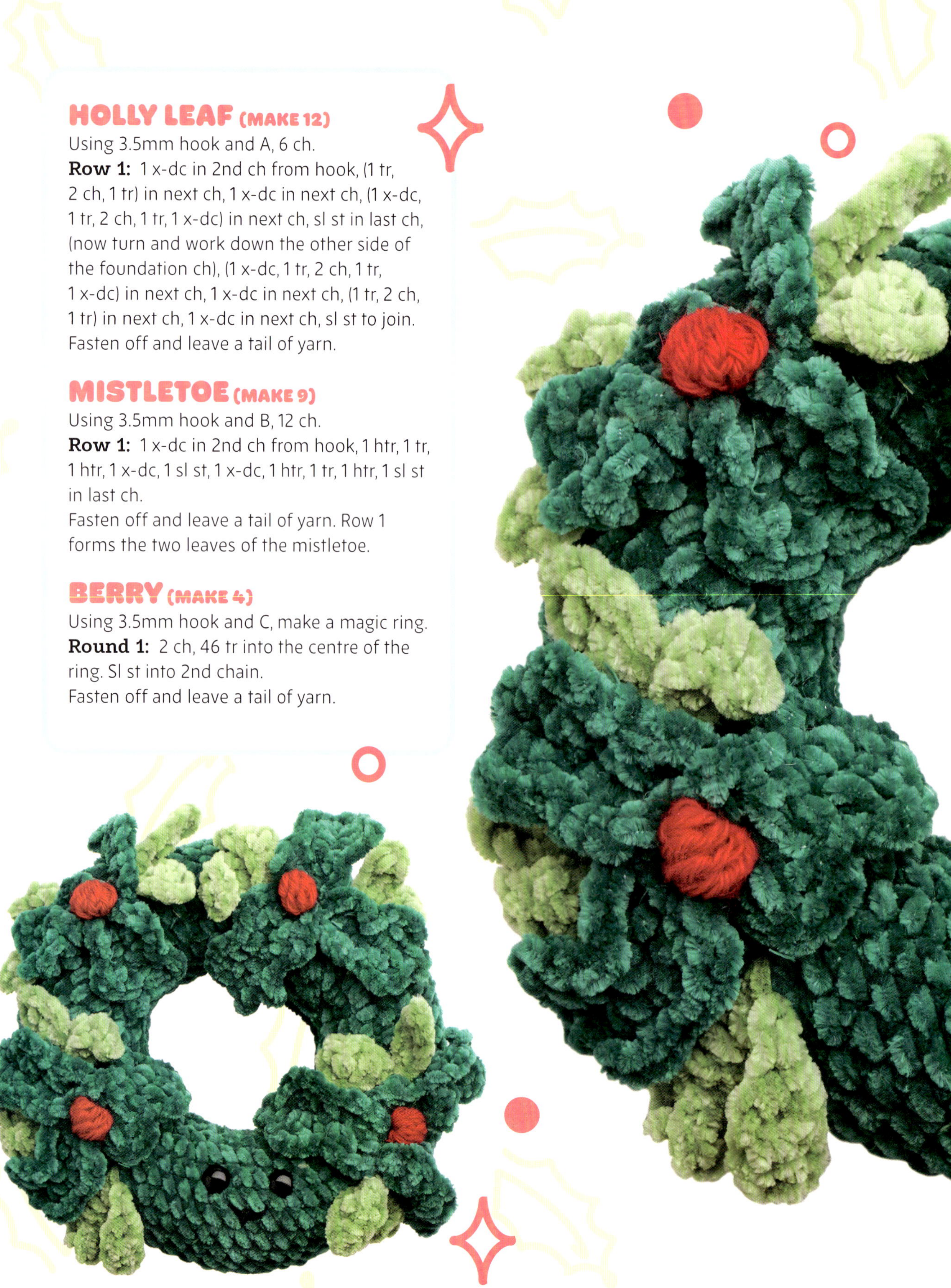

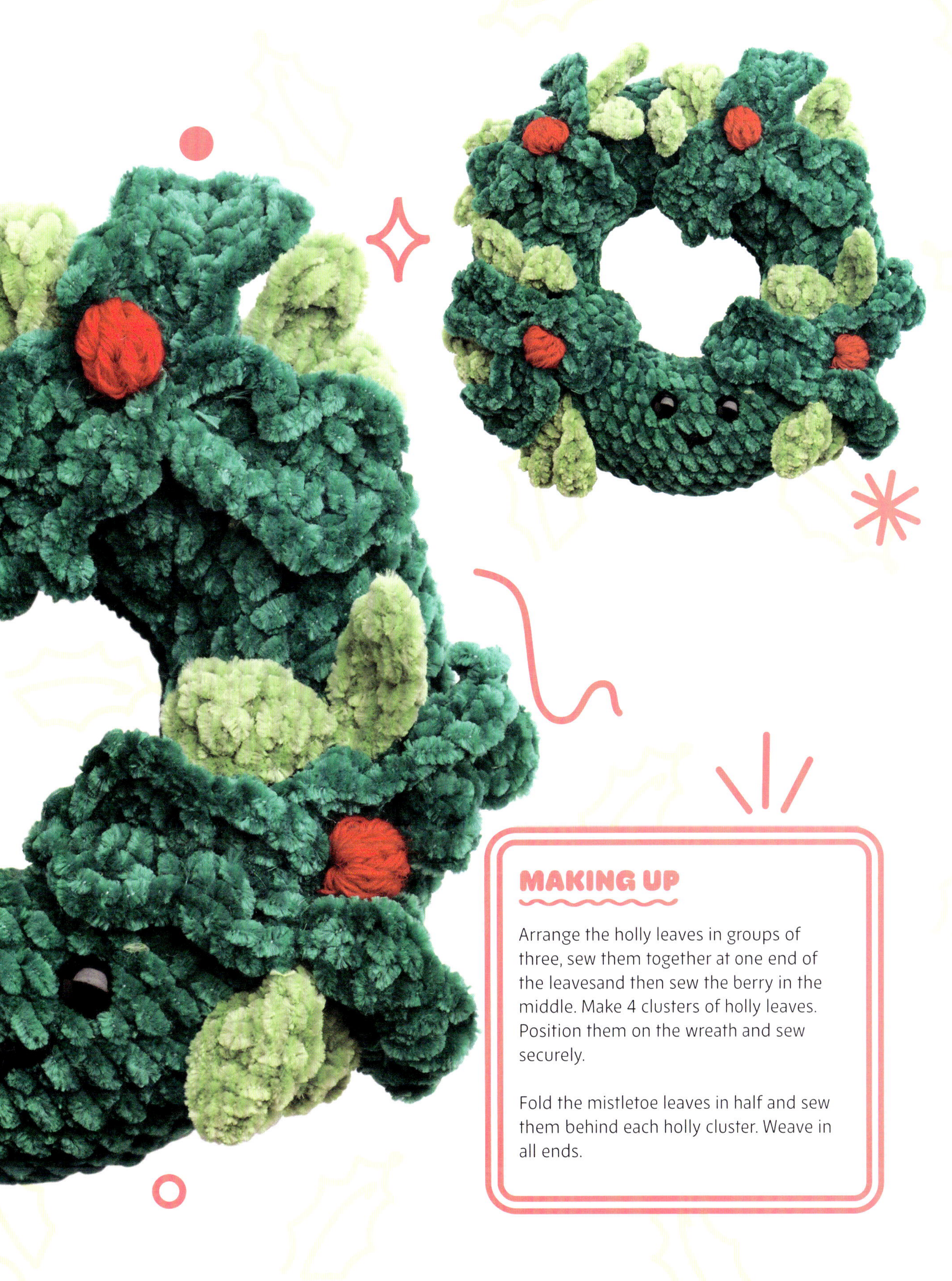

MAKING UP

Arrange the holly leaves in groups of three, sew them together at one end of the leavesand then sew the berry in the middle. Make 4 clusters of holly leaves. Position them on the wreath and sew securely.

Fold the mistletoe leaves in half and sew them behind each holly cluster. Weave in all ends.

CUDDLY CHRISTMAS TREE

What could be cuter than a cuddly Christmas tree? I have put a piece of card and some lentils in the base to weigh it down, but if you want to make this as a soft toy, just omit those and perhaps embroider the eyes. Why not add some mini pompoms, or even wind a small set of battery lights round the tree as a table decoration?

YOU WILL NEED

- **Stylecraft Squeeze Me DK, 100% polyester (219yd/200m per 100g ball): 1 x 100g ball in 5610 Emerald Green (A), a small amount of 5612 Chestnut Brown (B)**
- **DMC Lumina Metallic Thread, 60% viscose, 40% polyester (164yd/150m per 25g ball): A small amount of L3821 Gold (C)**
- **3.5mm (UK 9:US E/4) crochet hook**
- **Polyester stuffing**
- **Tapestry needle and stitch marker**
- **A pair of 3/8in (10mm) safety eyes**
- **A small piece of card**
- **A strand of black yarn**

FINISHED SIZE

The tree with trunk and star is approximately 8in (20cm) tall.

TECHNIQUES

Magic ring	dc2inc
Chain (ch)	dc2tog
Slip stitch (sl st)	Treble stitch (tr)
Cross double crochet (x-dc)	Back loop only (blo)

NOTE

The tree is worked in rounds, using the cross double crochet technique (see page 110). Place a marker at the beginning of each round so you know where you are in the pattern.

TREE

Using 3.5mm hook and A, make a magic ring.

Round 1: 1 ch, 4 dc into the centre of the ring.

Round 2: 2 x-dc into each st (8 sts).

Round 3: Work 1 round straight.

Round 4: (X-dc2inc, 1 x-dc) 4 times (12 sts).

Round 5: Work 1 round straight.

Round 6: (2 x-dc, x-dc2inc) 4 times (16 sts).

Round 7: Work 1 round straight.

Round 8: (3 x-dc, x-dc2inc) 4 times (20 sts).

Round 9: Work 1 round straight.

Round 10: (X-dc2inc, 4 x-dc) 4 times (24 sts).

Round 11: Work 1 round straight.

Round 12: (5 x-dc, x-dc2inc) 4 times (28 sts).

Round 13: Work 1 round straight.

Round 14: (6 x-dc, x-dc2inc) 4 times (32 sts).

Round 15: Work 1 round straight.

Round 16: (7 x-dc, x-dc2inc) 4 times (36 sts).

Round 17: Work 1 round straight.

Round 18: (8 x-dc, x-dc2inc) 4 times (40 sts).

Round 19: Work 1 round straight.

Round 20: (9 x-dc, x-dc2inc) 4 times (44 sts).

Round 21: Work 1 round straight.

Round 22: (10 x-dc, x-dc2inc) 4 times (48 sts).

Round 23: Work 1 round straight.

Round 24: 1 dc blo in each st (48 sts).

Round 25: (4 x-dc, x-dc2tog) 8 times (40 sts).

Round 26: (3 x-dc, x-dc2tog) 8 times (32 sts).

Round 27: (2 x-dc, x-dc2tog) 8 times (24 sts).

Round 28: (1 x-dc, x-dc2tog) 8 times (16 sts).

Round 29: (X-dc2tog) 8 times (8 sts).

Fasten off and weave in ends.

TRUNK

Using 3.5mm hook and B, make a magic ring.

Round 1: 1 ch, 8 x-dc into the centre of the ring.

Round 2: 2 x-dc into each st (16 sts).

Round 3: (1 x-dc, x-dc2inc) 8 times (24 sts).

Round 4: 1 x-dc blo in each st (24 sts).

Rounds 5–8: Work 4 rounds straight.

Fasten off and leave a tail of yarn.

STAR

Using 3.5mm hook and C, make a magic ring.

Round 1: (1 x-dc, 1 tr, 2ch 1 tr) into the centre of the ring 5 times, join with a sl st in 1st dc.

Pull the centre of the magic ring tight and using a tapestry needle secure with a small stitch.

MAKING UP

Using the photograph as a guide, position and secure safety eyes on the tree. Using the black yarn, embroider the mouth. Stuff the tree firmly.

Place a piece of card, approximately 1½in (3cm) in diameter, in the base of the trunk. Place some rice or lentils in a small bag or stocking and put in the trunk. Sew the top of the trunk to the base of the tree using small whip stitches (see page 122).

Sew the star firmly to the top of the tree.

CHEEKY CACTUS FAMILY

This pert plant looks great in a pot! I have turned the crochet material inside out to create a different texture and added a flower for detail.

YOU WILL NEED

- Scheepjes Stone Washed, 78% cotton, 22% acrylic (142yd/130m per 50g ball): 1 x 50g ball in 827 Peridot (A)
- Scheepjes Catona, 100% cotton (27yd/25m per 10g ball): 1 x 10g ball in 281 Tangerine (B)
- Stylecraft Special DK, 100% acrylic (323yd/295m per 100g ball): A small amount of 1054 Walnut (C)
- 3.5mm (UK 9:US E/4) crochet hook
- Tapestry needle
- Polyester stuffing

FINISHED SIZE

The large cactus is approximately 3¼in (8cm) tall.

TECHNIQUES

Magic ring
Chain (ch)
Slip stitch (sl st)
Double crochet (dc)
dc2inc
dc2tog

NOTE

The cactus is worked in spirals using the standard amigurumi technique, but turn remember to turn each piece inside out.

TALL CACTUS

Using 3.5mm hook and A, make a magic ring.
Round 1: 1 ch, 6 dc into the centre of the ring, join with a sl st.
Round 2: 2 dc into each st (12 sts).
Round 3: (3 dc, dc2inc) 3 times (15 sts).
Rounds 4–18: Work 15 rounds straight.
Fasten off and leave a tail of yarn.

MEDIUM CACTUS

Using 3.5mm hook and A, make a magic ring.
Round 1: 1 ch, 6 dc into the centre of the ring, join with a sl st.
Round 2: 2 dc into each st (12 sts).
Round 3: (3 dc, dc2inc) 3 times (15 sts).
Rounds 4–15: Work 12 rounds straight.
Fasten off and leave a tail of yarn.

SMALL CACTUS

Using 3.5mm hook and A, make a magic ring.
Round 1: 1 ch, 6 dc into the centre of the ring, join with a sl st.
Round 2: 2 dc into each st (12 sts).
Round 3: (3 dc, dc2inc) 3 times (15 sts).
Rounds 4–11: Work 8 rounds straight.
Fasten off and leave a tail of yarn.

FLOWER

Using 3.5mm hook and B, make a magic ring.
Round 1: 1 ch, 5 dc into the centre of the ring, join with a sl st.
Round 2: (4 ch, 1 sl st in next ch, sl st in same st) 5 times.
Fasten off and leave a tail of yarn.

SOIL

Using 3.5mm hook and C, make a magic ring.
Round 1: 1 ch, 6 dc into the centre of the ring.
Round 2: 2 dc into each st (12 sts).
Round 3: (1 dc, dc2inc) 6 times (18 sts).
Round 4: (2 dc, dc2inc) 6 times (24 sts).
Round 5: (3 dc, dc2inc) 6 times (30 sts).
Round 6: (4 dc, dc2inc) 6 times (36 sts).
Rounds 7–11: Work 5 rounds straight.
Round 12: (4 dc, dc2tog) 6 times (30 sts).
Round 13: (3 dc, dc2tog) 6 times (24 sts).
Round 14: (2 dc, dc2tog) 6 times (18 sts).
Stuff firmly with some stuffing.
Round 15: (1 dc, dc2tog) 6 times (12 sts).
Round 16: (Dc2tog) 6 times (6 sts).
Fasten off and weave in ends.

MAKING UP

Turn each cactus inside out. Weave in all ends at the top of the cactus. Using the photograph as a guide, place the safety eyes and use a strand of black yarn to create the features. Stuff each cactus firmly. Sew the flower bud onto the smallest cactus. Sew the base of each cactus to the top of the soil. Place into a small pot.

TEETERING TULIP

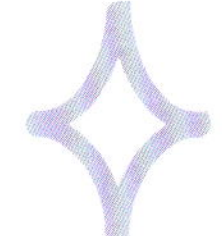

Who doesn't want a beautiful bunch of tulips? Make this dainty flower either as a single bloom in a pot with its leaf or as a group to make a bunch.

NOTE

This flower is made in the round using the amigurumi technique. I have created the stem by wrapping floristry wire with yarn and gluing the ends to ensure the yarn doesn't unravel (see page 121).

YOU WILL NEED

- **Scheepjes Metropolis, 75% wool, 25% nylon (219yd/200m per 50g ball): 1 x 50g ball in 052 Bangalore (A) and 032 Abu Dhabi (B). Other tulips use 047 Dubai, 055 Lima, 053 Santiago and 038 Brasov**
- **Stylecraft Special DK, 100% acrylic (323yd/295m per 100g ball): A small amount of 1054 Walnut (C)**
- **3mm (UK 11:US –) crochet hook**
- **3.5mm (UK 9:US E/4) crochet hook**
- **Tapestry needle**
- **Polyester stuffing**
- **A strand of black yarn**
- **2 x ⅛in (4mm) black safety eyes**
- **Floristry wire**
- **Craft glue**

FINISHED SIZE

The flower head is approximately 1¾in (4cm) wide. The flower on the stem is approximately 5in (12.5cm) tall.

TECHNIQUES

Magic ring	Double crochet (dc)
Chain (ch)	dc2inc
Slip stitch (sl st)	dc2tog

FLOWER

Using 3mm hook and A, make a magic ring.

Round 1: 1 ch, 6 dc into the centre of the ring, join with a sl st.

Round 2: (Dc2inc) 6 times (12 sts).

Round 3: (1 dc, dc2inc) 6 times (18 sts).

Round 4: (2 dc, dc2inc) 6 times (24 sts).

Round 5: (3 dc, dc2inc) 6 times (30 sts).

Rounds 6–15: Work 10 rounds straight.

Fasten off and leave a tail of yarn.

LEAF

Using 3mm hook and B, make a magic ring.

Round 1: 1 ch, 4 dc into the centre of the ring.

Round 2: (Dc2inc) 4 times (8 sts).

Round 3: (3 dc, dc2inc) twice (10 sts).

Round 4: (4 dc, dc2inc) twice (12 sts).

Rounds 5–19: Work 15 rounds straight.

Round 20: (4 dc, dc2tog) twice (10 sts).

Fasten off and leave a tail of yarn.

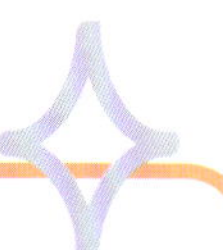

STEM

Cut a strand of floristry wire approximately 4in (10cm) long. Using B, leave a tail of yarn about 3½in (9cm) long and then start winding the yarn over the wire until the full length of the wire has been covered. Use a small amount of glue to secure the ends.

SOIL

Using 3.5mm hook and C, make a magic ring.
Round 1: 1 ch, 6 dc into the centre of the ring.
Round 2: 2 dc into each st (12 sts).
Round 3: (1 dc, dc2inc) 6 times (18 sts).
Round 4: (2 dc, dc2inc) 6 times (24 sts).
Round 5: (3 dc, dc2inc) 6 times (30 sts).
Round 6: (4 dc, dc2inc) 6 times (36 sts).
Rounds 7–11: Work 5 rounds straight.
Round 12: (4 dc, dc2tog) 6 times (30 sts).
Round 13: (3 dc, dc2tog) 6 times (24 sts).
Round 14: (2 dc, dc2tog) 6 times (18 sts).
Place a small bag of rice or lentils in the base and then stuff firmly with polyester stuffing.
Round 15: (1 dc, dc2tog) 6 times (12 sts).
Round 16: (Dc2tog) 6 times (6 sts).
Using a tapestry needle, weave this yarn through the last dc sts of the round and gather hole together. Fasten off and weave in ends.

MAKING UP

Using the photograph as a guide, place the plastic eyes and stitch the mouth using black yarn in the middle of the flower.

Poke the stem through the magic ring and use the starting tail of yarn to secure it to the stem. Place a little stuffing in the centre of the flower. Fold the top of the flower in half and then fold each half in half again to create four petal folds. Using the end tail of yarn, secure the centre of the folds.

Poke the stem into the centre of the soil. Place a small amount of floristry wire in the middle of the leaf. Fold the leaf in half at the base and then sew securely to the base of the stem. With a few small stitches, sew the base of the stem to the top of the soil. Place into a small pot.

DITSY DAISY

Daisies really are the happiest and most summery flowers. Sew a string of daisies together to make a flower crown or brighten your house with a single daisy in a vase.

NOTE

This flower is made by sewing five petals together and then sewing the centre face in the middle of the petals. Change your colours to create multicoloured versions of this classic flower.

YOU WILL NEED

- **Scheepjes Metropolis, 75% wool, 25% nylon (219yd/200m per 50g ball): 1 x 50g ball in 030 Toulouse (A), 038 Brasov (B) and 032 Abu Dhabi (C)**
- **Stylecraft Special DK, 100% acrylic (323yd/295m per 100g ball): A small amount of 1054 Walnut (D)**
- **3mm (UK 11:US –) crochet hook**
- **3.5mm (UK 9:US E/4) crochet hook**
- **Tapestry needle**
- **Small bag of rice or lentils**
- **Polyester stuffing**
- **A strand of black yarn**
- **2 x ⅛in (4mm) black safety eyes**
- **Chenille wire**

FINISHED SIZE

The flower head is approximately 3¾in (9cm) wide. The flower on the stem is approximately 5in (12cm) tall.

TECHNIQUES

Magic ring
Chain (ch)
Slip stitch (sl st)
Double crochet (dc)
dc2inc
dc2tog

PETAL (MAKE 5)

Using 3mm hook and A, make a magic ring.
Round 1: 1 ch, 6 dc into the centre of the ring, join with a sl st.
Round 2: (Dc2inc) 6 times (12 sts).
Round 3: (1 dc, dc2inc) 6 times (18 sts).
Rounds 4–6: Work 3 rounds straight.
Round 7: (7 dc, dc2tog) twice (16 sts).
Round 8: (6 dc, dc2tog) twice (14 sts).
Round 9: (5 dc, dc2tog) twice (12 sts).
Fasten off and leave a tail of yarn.

FLOWER FACE

Using 3mm hook and B, make a magic ring.
Round 1: 1 ch, 8 dc into the centre of the ring, join with a sl st.
Round 2: (Dc2inc) 8 times (16 sts).
Round 3: (1 dc, dc2inc) 8 times (24 sts).
Rounds 4–5: Work 2 rounds straight.
Fasten off and leave a tail of yarn.

FLOWER BACK

Using 3mm hook and C, make a magic ring.
Round 1: 1 ch, 6 dc into the centre of the ring, join with a sl st.
Round 2: (Dc2inc) 6 times (12 sts).
Round 3: (1 dc, dc2inc) 6 times (18 sts).
Fasten off and leave a tail of yarn.

STEM

Using 3mm hook and C, ch 4 sts, sl st in 1st ch to create a loop.
Round 1: 1 ch, 4 dc into the centre of the loop.
Rounds 2–16: Work 15 rounds straight (4 sts).
Fasten off and leave a tail of yarn.

LEAF (MAKE 2)

Using 3mm hook and C, make a magic ring.
Round 1: 1 ch, 4 dc into the centre of the ring.
Round 2: (Dc2inc) 4 times (8 sts).
Round 3: (3 dc, dc2inc) twice (10 sts).
Round 4: (4 dc, dc2inc) twice (12 sts).
Rounds 5–6: Work 2 rounds straight.
Round 7: (4 dc, dc2tog) twice (10 sts).
Round 8: (3dc, dc2tog) twice (8 sts).
Round 9: (Dc2tog) 4 times (4 sts).
Fasten off and leave a tail of yarn.

SOIL

Using 3.5mm hook and D, make a magic ring.
Round 1: 1 ch, 6 dc into the centre of the ring.
Round 2: 2 dc into each st (12 sts).
Round 3: (1 dc, dc2inc) 6 times (18 sts).
Round 4: (2 dc, dc2inc) 6 times (24 sts).
Round 5: (3 dc, dc2inc) 6 times (30 sts).
Round 6: (4 dc, dc2inc) 6 times (36 sts).
Rounds 7–11: Work 5 rounds straight.
Round 12: (4 dc, dc2tog) 6 times (30 sts).
Round 13: (3 dc, dc2tog) 6 times (24 sts).
Round 14: (2 dc, dc2tog) 6 times (18 sts).
Place a small bag of rice or lentils in the base and then stuff firmly with polyester stuffing.
Round 15: (1 dc, dc2tog) 6 times (12 sts).
Round 16: (Dc2tog) 6 times (6 sts).
Using a tapestry needle, weave this yarn through the last dc sts of the round and gather hole together. Fasten off and weave in ends.

MAKING UP

Fold each petal in half and press it flat with your hand. Arrange the six petals to form a star and, using the tail of yarn, sew the end rows together to form a flat star. Using the photograph as a guide, place the plastic eyes on the face and stitch the mouth using black yarn. Sew the face on the front of the flower.

Fold a chenille wire in half and then feed this through the middle of the flower stem. Position the stem so that it meets the centre back of the flower. Place the flower back over the top of the stem. Use the yarn tail to whip stitch (see page 122) the flower back to the back of the petals.

Poke the stem into the centre of the soil. Sew the base of each leaf to the base of the stem. With a few small stitches, sew the base of the stem to the top of the soil. Place into a small pot.

JOYFUL SUNFLOWER

What a cheerful flower! Who wouldn't want this little cutie sitting on their beside table or on their desk?

NOTE

This flower uses cross double crochet (see page 110) to create the texture of the raised centre (the seeds) and treble and double trebles to create the petals.

YOU WILL NEED

- **Stylecraft Special DK, 100% acrylic (323yd/295m per 100g ball): A small amount of 1054 Walnut (A), 1856 Dandelion (B) and 1852 Apple (C)**
- **3mm (UK 11:US –) crochet hook**
- **3.5mm (UK 9:US E/4) crochet hook**
- **Tapestry needle**
- **Small bag of rice or lentils**
- **Polyester stuffing**
- **White felt**
- **A strand of pink yarn**
- **2 x 5⁄16in (8mm) black safety eyes**
- **Chenille wire**

FINISHED SIZE

The flower head is approximately 3½in (9cm) wide. The flower on the stem is approximately 5in (12cm) tall.

TECHNIQUES

Magic ring
Chain (ch)
Slip stitch (sl st)
Double crochet (dc)
dc2inc
dc2tog
Cross double crochet (x-dc)
Double treble (dtr)
Back loop only (blo)

FLOWER SEEDS AND PETALS

Using 3mm hook and A, make a magic ring.
Use cross double crochet for rounds 2–6.

Round 1: 1 ch, 8 dc into the centre of the ring, join with a sl st.
Round 2: (X-dc2inc) 8 times (16 sts).
Round 3: (1 x-dc, x-dc2inc) 8 times (24 sts).
Round 4: (2 x-dc, x-dc2inc) 8 times (32 sts).
Rounds 5–6: Work 2 rounds straight in x-dc.
Fasten off A.
Round 7: Change to B with a sl st, work blo, *(1 tr, 2 dtr, 2 ch, sl st in 1st ch) in next st, (2 dtr, 1 tr) in next st, 1 sl st in next 2 sts; rep from * 7 times (8 petals).
Fasten off and leave a tail of yarn.

FLOWER BACK

Using 3mm hook and C, make a magic ring.
Round 1: 1 ch, 8 dc into the centre of the ring, join with a sl st.
Round 2: (Dc2inc) 8 times (16 sts).
Round 3: (1 dc, dc2inc) 8 times (24 sts).
Round 4: (2 dc, dc2inc) 8 times (32 sts).
Round 5: Work 1 round straight.
Fasten off and leave a tail of yarn.

STEM

Using 3mm hook and yarn C, 4 ch, sl st in 1st ch to create a loop.

Round 1: 1 ch, 5 dc into the centre of the loop.

Rounds 2–16: Work 15 rounds straight (5 sts).

Fasten off and leave a tail of yarn.

LEAF (MAKE 2)

Using 3.5mm hook and yarn C, 8 ch.

Row 1: 1 dc in 2nd ch, 1 htr, 1 tr, 2 tr in next st, 1 tr, 1 htr, 1 dc in last ch, 2 ch, (now turn and work down the other side of the foundation ch), 1 dc, 1 htr, 1 tr, 2 tr in next ch, 1 tr, 1 htr, 1 dc, 1 sl st in 1st ch.

Fasten off and leave a tail of yarn.

SOIL

Using 3.5mm hook and A, make a magic ring.

Round 1: 1 ch, 6 dc into the centre of the ring.

Round 2: 2 dc into each st (12 sts).

Round 3: (1 dc, dc2inc) 6 times (18 sts).

Round 4: (2 dc, dc2inc) 6 times (24 sts).

Round 5: (3 dc, dc2inc) 6 times (30 sts).

Round 6: (4 dc, dc2inc) 6 times (36 sts).

Rounds 7–11: Work 5 rounds straight.

Round 12: (4 dc, dc2tog) 6 times (30 sts).

Round 13: (3 dc, dc2tog) 6 times (24 sts).

Round 14: (2 dc, dc2tog) 6 times (18 sts).

Place a small bag of rice or lentils in the base and then stuff firmly with polyester stuffing.

Round 15: (1 dc, dc2tog) 6 times (12 sts).

Round 16: (Dc2tog) 6 times (6 sts).

Using a tapestry needle, weave this yarn through the last dc sts of the round and gather hole together. Fasten off and weave in ends.

MAKING UP

Weave in the ends of the flower seeds and petals.

Take two small pieces of white felt. Make a small hole in the centre of each piece and poke the shank of the safety eye through the centre. Using small scissors, trim the felt so that it is just a little larger than the black plastic circle of the eye. Then, using the photograph as a guide, position and secure the safety eyes on the seeds of the flower. Stitch the mouth using the pink yarn. Use a small amount of stuffing to stuff the back of the seeds.

Fold a chenille wire in half and then feed this through the middle of the flower stem. Position the stem so that it meets the centre back of the flower. Place the flower back over the stuffing and the top of the stem. Use the yarn tail to whip stitch (see page 122) the flower back to the stitches at the base of the petals.

Poke the stem into the centre of the soil. With a few small stitches, sew the base of the stem to the top of the soil. Use the long tails of yarn C to sew the base of the leaves securely to the top of the soil. Place into a small pot (see pages 124–5).

PLAYFUL POPPY

This flower is so delicate; its petals appear to be made out of paper. Try making some poppies in a range of vibrant shades.

NOTE

The fronds of the poppy are made by working slip stitches back along lengths of chain stitches.

YOU WILL NEED

- **Stylecraft Special DK, 100% acrylic (323yd/295m per 100g ball): A small amount of 1246 Lipstick (A), 1852 Apple (B) and 1054 Walnut (C)**
- **Scheepjes Catona, 100% cotton (27yd/25m per 10g ball): 1 x 10g ball in 110 Jet Black (D)**
- **3mm (UK 11:US –) crochet hook**
- **3.5mm (UK 9:US E/4) crochet hook**
- **Tapestry needle and stitch marker**
- **Small bag of rice or lentils**
- **Polyester stuffing**
- **2 x 5⁄16in (8mm) black safety eyes**
- **Chenille wire**
- **A small fork**

FINISHED SIZE

The flower head is approximately 3½in (9cm) wide. The flower with stem is 4in (10cm) tall.

TECHNIQUES

Magic ring
Chain (ch)
Slip stitch (sl st)
Double crochet (dc)
Half treble (htr)
Back loop only (blo)

LARGE PETAL (MAKE 2)

Using 3.5mm hook and A, 12 ch.
Round 1: 1 dc in 2nd ch from hook, 10 dc to end, 1 ch. Now work on the other side of the ch sts: 11 dc, 1 ch (22 sts). You will now work in spirals.
Round 2: Place marker, dc2inc, 9 dc, dc2inc, dc2inc in turning ch, dc2inc, 9 dc, dc2inc, dc2inc in turning ch (30 sts).
Rounds 3–4: Work 2 rounds straight.
Round 5: Place marker, dc2tog, 3 dc, dc2tog, 4 dc, dc2tog 3 times, 3 dc, dc2tog, 4 dc, dc2tog twice (22 sts).
Round 6: Work 1 round straight.
Round 7: Place marker, dc2tog, 2 dc, dc2tog, 2 dc, dc2tog twice, 2 dc, dc2tog, 2 dc, dc2tog twice (15 sts).
Round 8: Place marker, dc2tog, 1 dc, dc2tog, 1 dc, dc2tog, 1 dc, dc2tog, 1 dc, dc2tog, 1 dc (10 sts).
Fasten off and leave a tail of yarn.

SMALL PETAL (MAKE 2)

Using 3.5mm hook and A, 8 ch.
Round 1: 1 dc in 2nd ch from hook, 6 dc to end, 1 ch. Now work on the other side of the ch sts: 7 dc, 1 ch (14 sts). You will now work in spirals.
Round 2: Place marker, dc2inc, 5 dc, dc2inc, dc2inc in turning ch, dc2inc, 5 dc, dc2inc, dc2inc in turning ch (22 sts).
Rounds 3–4: Work 2 rounds straight.
Round 5: Place marker, dc2tog, 2 dc, dc2tog, 1 dc, dc2tog 3 times, 2 dc, dc2tog, 1 dc, dc2tog twice (14 sts).
Round 6: Work 1 round straight.
Round 7: Place marker, (dc2tog, 1 dc) 4 times, 2 dc (10 sts).
Round 8: Work 1 row straight.
Fasten off and leave a tail of yarn.

FLOWER FACE

Using 3mm hook and B, make a magic ring.
Round 1: 1 ch, 6 dc into the centre of the ring, join with a sl st.
Round 2: (Dc2inc) 6 times (12 sts).
Round 3: (1 dc, dc2inc) 6 times (18 sts).
Round 4: 1 dc blo in each st (18 sts).
Round 5: (1 dc, dc2tog) 6 times (12 sts).
Fasten off and leave a tail of yarn.

FLOWER BACK

Using 3mm hook and B, make a magic ring.
Round 1: 1 ch, 8 dc into the centre of the ring, join with a sl st.
Round 2: (Dc2inc) 8 times (16 sts).
Round 3: (1 dc, dc2inc) 8 times (24 sts).
Round 4: (2 dc, dc2inc) 8 times (32 sts).
Round 5: Work 1 round straight.
Fasten off and leave a tail of yarn.

STEM

Using 3mm hook and B, 4 ch, sl st in 1st ch to create a loop.

Round 1: 1 ch, 5 dc into the centre of the loop.

Rounds 2–16: Work 15 rounds straight (5 sts).

Fasten off and leave a tail of yarn.

LEAF

Using 3mm hook and B, 5 ch.

Round 1: Sl st in 2nd ch from hook, 3 sl st, 3 ch, sl st in 2nd ch from hook, 1 sl st, 5 ch, sl st in 2nd ch from hook, 1 sl st, 3 ch, sl st in 2nd ch from hook, 1 sl st, 3 ch, sl st in 2nd ch from hook, 1 sl st, 1 sl st in each of next 2 ch, 3 ch, sl st in 2nd ch from hook, 1 sl st, sl st into 1st starting ch (6 fronds).

Fasten off and leave a tail of yarn.

SOIL

Using 3.5mm hook and C, make a magic ring.

Round 1: 1 ch, 6 dc into the centre of the ring.

Round 2: 2 dc into each st (12 sts).

Round 3: (1 dc, dc2inc) 6 times (18 sts).

Round 4: (2 dc, dc2inc) 6 times (24 sts).

Round 5: (3 dc, dc2inc) 6 times (30 sts).

Round 6: (4 dc, dc2inc) 6 times (36 sts).

Rounds 7–11: Work 5 rounds straight.

Round 12: (4 dc, dc2tog) 6 times (30 sts).

Round 13: (3 dc, dc2tog) 6 times (24 sts).

Round 14: (2 dc, dc2tog) 6 times (18 sts).

Place a small bag of rice or lentils in the base and then stuff firmly with polyester stuffing.

Round 15: (1 dc, dc2tog) 6 times (12 sts).

Round 16: (Dc2tog) 6 times (6 sts).

Using a tapestry needle, weave this yarn through the last dc sts of the round and gather hole together. Fasten off and weave in ends.

STAMENS

Using D, use the technique to make a thin pompom (see page 123) by winding the yarn over the end of a small fork about 10 times. Secure with a 4in (10cm) strand of yarn in the centre and cut the sides of the wrapped yarn.

MAKING UP

Fold each petal in half and press it flat with your hand. Arrange the two large petals so they are opposite each other, and, using the tail of yarn, sew the end rows together. Do the same for the small petals and then sew the small petals on top of the large petals. Flatten the stamen pompom. Sew the pompom firmly to the centre of the poppy.

Using the photograph as a guide, place the plastic eyes and stitch the mouth using black yarn on the face. Sew the face in the centre of the stamen pompom.

Fold a chenille wire in half and then feed this through the middle of the flower stem. Position the stem so that it meets the centre back of the flower. Place the flower back over the top of the stem.

Poke the stem into the centre of the soil. Sew the base of the leaf to the bottom of the stem. With a few small stitches, sew the base of the stem to the top of the soil. Place into a small pot.

SUNNY DAFFODIL

Spring has arrived when the nodding yellow heads of the daffodils appear. Their cheery faces brighten our day.

NOTE

This flower is made by sewing six petals together and then sewing the centre face and frill in the middle of the petals.

YOU WILL NEED

- **Scheepjes Metropolis, 75% wool, 25% nylon (219yd/200m per 50g ball): 1 x 50g ball in 038 Brasov (A) and 032 Abu Dhabi (B)**
- **Stylecraft Special DK, 100% acrylic (323yd/295m per 100g ball): A small amount of 1054 Walnut (C)**
- **3mm (UK 11:US –) crochet hook**
- **3.5mm (UK 9:US E/4) crochet hook**
- **Tapestry needle**
- **Small bag of rice or lentils**
- **Polyester stuffing**
- **A strand of black yarn**
- **2 x ⅛in (4mm) black safety eyes**
- **Chenille wire**
- **Floristry wire**

FINISHED SIZE

The flower head is approximately 4in (10cm) wide. The flower on the stem is approximately 4½in (12cm) tall.

TECHNIQUES

Magic ring
Chain (ch)
Slip stitch (sl st)
Double crochet (dc)
dc2inc
dc2tog
Double treble (dtr)
Back loop only (blo)
Front loop only (flo)

PETALS (MAKE 6)

Using 3mm hook and A, make a magic ring.

Round 1: 1 ch, 4 dc into the centre of the ring.

Round 2: (Dc2inc) 4 times (8 sts).

Round 3: (3 dc, dc2inc) twice (10 sts).

Round 4: (4 dc, dc2inc) twice (12 sts).

Rounds 5–7: Work 3 rounds straight.

Round 8: (4 dc, dc2tog) twice (10 sts).

Round 9: (3 dc, dc2tog) twice (8 sts).

Fasten off and leave a tail of yarn.

FLOWER FACE

Using 3mm hook and A, make a magic ring.

Round 1: 1 ch, 6 dc into the centre of the ring, join with a sl st.

Round 2: (Dc2inc) 6 times (12 sts).

Round 3: (1 dc, dc2inc) 6 times (18 sts).

Round 4: 1 dc blo in each st (18 sts).

Round 5: (1 dc, dc2tog) 6 times (12 sts).

Frill round: Join A to any front loop of round 3 with a sl st, (3 ch, 2 dtr flo) in same st, *3 dtr flo in next st; rep from * 16 times, join with a sl st to top of 3rd ch (54 sts).

Fasten off and leave a tail of yarn.

FLOWER BACK

Using 3mm hook and B, make a magic ring.

Round 1: 1 ch, 6 dc into the centre of the ring, join with a sl st.

Round 2: (Dc2inc) 6 times (12 sts).

Round 3: (1 dc, dc2inc) 6 times (18 sts).

Fasten off and leave a tail of yarn.

STEM

Using 3mm hook and B, 4 ch, sl st in 1st ch to create a loop.

Round 1: 1 ch, 4 dc into the centre of the loop.

Rounds 2–16: Work 15 rounds straight (4 sts).

Fasten off and leave a tail of yarn.

LEAF

Using 3mm hook and B, make a magic ring.
Round 1: 1 ch, 4 dc into the centre of the ring.
Round 2: (1 dc, dc2inc) twice (6 sts).
Round 3: (2 dc, dc2inc) twice (8 sts).
Continue to work straight until your leaf measures 2¼in (6cm).
Next round: (2 dc, dc2tog) twice (6 sts).
Fasten off and leave a tail of yarn.

SOIL

Using 3.5mm hook and C, make a magic ring.
Round 1: 1 ch, 6 dc into the centre of the ring.
Round 2: 2 dc into each st (12 sts).
Round 3: (1 dc, dc2inc) 6 times (18 sts).
Round 4: (2 dc, dc2inc) 6 times (24 sts).
Round 5: (3 dc, dc2inc) 6 times (30 sts).
Round 6: (4 dc, dc2inc) 6 times (36 sts).
Rounds 7–11: Work 5 rounds straight.
Round 12: (4 dc, dc2tog) 6 times (30 sts).
Round 13: (3 dc, dc2tog) 6 times (24 sts).
Round 14: (2 dc, dc2tog) 6 times (18 sts).
Place a small bag of rice or lentils in the base and then stuff firmly with polyester stuffing.
Round 15: (1 dc, dc2tog) 6 times (12 sts).
Round 16: (Dc2tog) 6 times (6 sts).
Using a tapestry needle, weave this yarn through the last dc sts of the round and gather hole together. Fasten off and weave in ends.

MAKING UP

Fold each petal in half and press it flat with your hand. Arrange the six petals to form a star and, using the tail of yarn, sew the end rows together to form a flat star. Using the photograph as a guide, place the plastic eyes and stitch the mouth on the face using black yarn. Sew the face in the centre of the petals.

Fold a chenille wire in half and then feed this through the middle of the flower stem. Position the stem so that it meets the centre back of the flower. Place the flower back over the top of the stem. Use the yarn tail to whip stitch (see page 122) the flower back to the stitches at the base of the petals.

Poke the stem into the centre of the soil. Place a piece of floristry wire in the leaf so that you can bend and arrange it as you like. Sew the base of the leaf to the bottom of the stem. With a few small stitches, sew the base of the stem to the top of the soil. Place into a small pot (see pages 124–5).

PRETTY PANSY

Pansies always look like a host of pretty faces looking at you from the garden.

YOU WILL NEED

- **Scheepjes Metropolis, 75% wool, 25% nylon (219yd/200m per 50g ball): 1 x 50g ball in 003 Dallas (A), 038 Brasov (B) and 032 Abu Dhabi (C)**
- **Stylecraft Special DK, 100% acrylic (323yd/295m per 100g ball): A small amount of 1054 Walnut (D)**
- **3mm (UK 11:US –) crochet hook**
- **3.5mm (UK 9:US E/4) crochet hook**
- **Tapestry needle**
- **Small bag of rice or lentils**
- **Polyester stuffing**
- **A strand of black yarn**
- **2 x ⅛in (4mm) black safety eyes**
- **Chenille wire**

FINISHED SIZE

The flower head is approximately 2¼in (6cm) wide. The flower on the stem is approximately 5¼in (13cm) tall.

TECHNIQUES

Magic ring	Double crochet (dc)
Chain (ch)	dc2inc
Slip stitch (sl st)	dc2tog

NOTE

This flower is made by sewing five petals together and then sewing the flower face to the middle of the petals. Get inspiration from nature to choose from a wide range of different colours for your pansies.

PLAIN PETAL

(MAKE 2 IN A AND 1 IN B)

Using 3mm hook make a magic ring.
Round 1: 1 ch, 6 dc into the centre of the ring, join with a sl st.
Round 2: (Dc2inc) 6 times (12 sts).
Round 3: (1 dc, dc2inc) 6 times (18 sts).
Rounds 4–5: Work 2 rounds straight.
Round 6: (7 dc, dc2tog) twice (16 sts).
Round 7: (6 dc, dc2tog) twice (14 sts).
Round 8: (5 dc, dc2tog) twice (12 sts).
Round 9: (4 dc, dc2tog) twice (10 sts).
Fasten off and leave a tail of yarn.

TWO-TONE PETAL (MAKE 2)

Using 3mm hook and A, make a magic ring.
Round 1: 1 ch, 6 dc into the centre of the ring, join with a sl st.
Round 2: (Dc2inc) 6 times (12 sts).
Round 3: (1 dc, dc2inc) 6 times (18 sts).
Fasten off A.
Rounds 4–5: Change to yarn B.
Work 2 rounds straight.
Round 6: (7 dc, dc2tog) twice (16 sts).
Round 7: (6 dc, dc2tog) twice (14 sts).
Round 8: (5 dc, dc2tog) twice (12 sts).
Round 9: (4 dc, dc2tog) twice (10 sts).
Fasten off and leave a tail of yarn.

FLOWER FACE

Using 3mm hook and B, make a magic ring.
Round 1: Ch 1, 6 dc into the centre of the ring, join with a sl st.
Round 2: (Dc2inc) 6 times (12 sts).
Round 3: (1 dc, dc2inc) 6 times (18 sts).
Fasten off and leave a tail of yarn.

FLOWER BACK

Using 3mm hook and C, make a magic ring.
Round 1: 1 ch, 6 dc into the centre of the ring, join with a sl st.
Round 2: (Dc2inc) 6 times (12 sts).
Round 3: (1 dc, dc2inc) 6 times (18 sts).
Fasten off and leave a tail of yarn.

STEM

Using 3mm hook and yarn C, 4 ch, sl st in 1st ch to create a loop.
Round 1: 1 ch, 4 dc into the centre of the loop.
Rounds 2–16: Work 15 rounds straight (4 sts).
Fasten off and leave a tail of yarn.

LEAF (MAKE 3)

Using 3mm hook and C, make a magic ring.
Round 1: 1 ch, 6 dc into the centre of the ring, join with a sl st.
Round 2: (Dc2inc) 6 times (12 sts).
Rounds 3–5: Work 3 rounds straight.
Round 6: (4 dc, dc2tog) twice (10 sts).
Round 7: (3 dc, dc2tog) twice (8 sts).
Round 8: (2 dc, dc2tog) twice (6 sts).
Fasten off and leave a tail of yarn.

SOIL

Using 3.5mm hook and D, make a magic ring.
Round 1: 1 ch, 6 dc into the centre of the ring.
Round 2: 2 dc into each st (12 sts).
Round 3: (1 dc, dc2inc) 6 times (18 sts).
Round 4: (2 dc, dc2inc) 6 times (24 sts).
Round 5: (3 dc, dc2inc) 6 times (30 sts).
Round 6: (4 dc, dc2inc) 6 times (36 sts).
Rounds 7–11: Work 5 rounds straight.
Round 12: (4 dc, dc2tog) 6 times (30 sts).
Round 13: (3 dc, dc2tog) 6 times (24 sts).
Round 14: (2 dc, dc2tog) 6 times (18 sts).
Place a small bag of rice or lentils in the base and then stuff firmly with polyester stuffing.
Round 15: (1 dc, dc2tog) 6 times (12 sts).
Round 16: (Dc2tog) 6 times (6 sts).
Using a tapestry needle, weave this yarn through the last dc sts of the round and gather hole together. Fasten off and weave in ends.

MAKING UP

Fold each petal in half and press it flat with your hand. Place the two top petals so they overlap, then place the two-tone petals at right angles on top. Finally, place the bottom petal on top. Using the tail of yarn, sew the end rows together to form the flower shape.

Using the photograph as a guide, place the plastic eyes and stitch the mouth on the face using black yarn. Sew the face on the front of the flower.

Fold a chenille wire in half and then feed this through the middle of the flower stem. Position the stem so that it meets the centre back of the flower. Place the flower back over the top of the stem. Use the yarn tail to whip stitch (see page 122) the flower back to the back of the petals.

Poke the stem into the centre of the soil. Sew the base of each leaf to the middle of the stem. With a few small stitches, sew the base of the stem to the top of the soil. Place into a small pot.

ROSY ROSE

Ah, the most romantic of flowers. Giving this rose means your love will never die. Plus, its cheeky face will please anyone who receives it.

YOU WILL NEED

- Drops Alpaca 4ply, 100% alpaca (183yd/167m per 50g ball):
  1 x 50g ball in 9034 Rose Petal (A) and 7815 Forest Mix (B)
- Stylecraft Special DK, 100% acrylic (323yd/295m per 100g ball):
  A small amount of 1054 Walnut (C)
- 3mm (UK 11:US –) crochet hook
- 3.5mm (UK 9:US E/4) crochet hook
- Tapestry needle
- Small bag of rice or lentils
- Polyester stuffing
- A strand of black yarn
- 2 x ⅛in (4mm) black safety eyes
- Chenille wire

FINISHED SIZE

The flower head is approximately 2¼in (6cm) wide. The flower on the stem is approximately 5in (12.5cm) tall.

TECHNIQUES

Magic ring
Chain (ch)
Slip stitch (sl st)
Double crochet (dc)
dc2inc
dc2tog
Treble crochet (tr)

NOTE

This flower is made by sewing five petals together and then sewing the centre face in the middle of the petals. I've chosen a lovely bright red pot for this rose – see pages 124–5 for instructions.

FRONT PETALS

Using 3mm hook and A, 30 ch.

Row 1: 1 dc in 4th ch from hook, (3 ch, skip 1 ch, sl st in next st) 13 times, turn (14 petals).

Row 2: * (1 dc, 3 tr, 1 dc) in next ch sp; rep from * 13 times. Fasten off and weave in ends.

BACK PETALS

Using 3mm hook and A, 18 ch, sl st in 1st ch to form a loop.

Row 1: 1 dc in the centre of the loop, * 4 ch, 5 tr in centre of the loop, 4 ch, sl st in centre of the loop; rep from * 4 times (5 petals). Fasten off and weave in ends.

FLOWER FACE

Using 3mm hook and A, make a magic ring.

Round 1: 1 ch, 8 dc into the centre of the ring, join with a sl st.

Round 2: (Dc2inc) 8 times (16 sts).

Round 3: (1 dc, dc2inc) 8 times (24 sts).

Rounds 4–5: Work 2 rounds straight.

Fasten off and leave a tail of yarn.

FLOWER BACK

Using 3mm hook and B, make a magic ring.

Round 1: 1 ch, 6 dc into the centre of the ring, join with a sl st.

Round 2: (Dc2inc) 6 times (12 sts).

Round 3: (1 dc, dc2inc) 6 times (18 sts).

Fasten off and leave a tail of yarn.

STEM

Using 3mm hook and B, 4 ch, sl st in 1st ch to create a loop.

Round 1: 1 ch, 4 dc into the centre of the loop.

Rounds 2–18: Work 17 rounds straight (4 sts).

Fasten off and leave a tail of yarn.

LEAF

Using 3mm hook and B, make a magic ring.

Round 1: 1 ch, 4 dc into the centre of the ring.

Round 2: (Dc2inc) 4 times (8 sts).

Round 3: (3 dc, dc2inc) twice (10 sts).

Round 4: (4 dc, dc2inc) twice (12 sts).

Rounds 5–6: Work 2 rounds straight.

Round 7: (4 dc, dc2tog) twice (10 sts).

Round 8: (3 dc, dc2tog) twice (8 sts).

Round 9: (Dc2tog) 4 times (4 sts).

Fasten off and leave a tail of yarn.

SOIL

Using 3.5mm hook and C, make a magic ring.

Round 1: 1 ch, 6 dc into the centre of the ring.

Round 2: 2 dc into each st (12 sts).

Round 3: (1 dc, dc2inc) 6 times (18 sts).

Round 4: (2 dc, dc2inc) 6 times (24 sts).

Round 5: (3 dc, dc2inc) 6 times (30 sts).

Round 6: (4 dc, dc2inc) 6 times (36 sts).

Rounds 7–11: Work 5 rounds straight.

Round 12: (4 dc, dc2tog) 6 times (30 sts).

Round 13: (3 dc, dc2tog) 6 times (24 sts).

Round 14: (2 dc, dc2tog) 6 times (18 sts).

Place a small bag of rice or lentils in the base and then stuff firmly with polyester stuffing.

Round 15: (1 dc, dc2tog) 6 times (12 sts).

Round 16: (Dc2tog) 6 times (6 sts).

Using a tapestry needle, weave this yarn through the last dc sts of the round and gather hole together. Fasten off and weave in ends.

MAKING UP

Using the photograph as a guide, place the plastic eyes and stitch the mouth on the face using black yarn. Sew the face on the front of the flower. Take the front petals. roll them around the outside of the face and sew small stitches to keep them in place. You should have around two rows of petals. Turn your flower over so the back is facing you. With RS facing, take the back petals and sew to the back of the flower using small whip stitches (see page 122).

Fold a chenille wire in half and then feed this through the middle of the flower stem. Position the stem so that it meets the centre back of the flower. Place the flower back over the top of the stem. Use the yarn tail to whip stitch the flower back to the back of the petals.

Poke the stem into the centre of the soil. Sew the base of the leaf to the base to the stem approximately ¾in (2cm) below the flower. With a few small stitches, sew the base of the stem to the top of the soil. Place into a small pot (see pages 124–5).

DARLING DAHLIA

Dahlias are a new favourite in my garden. The splashy blooms come in a wide range of vibrant colours and have such a glamorous impact.

NOTE

This flower is made by creating a grid-like base which you then work on to place the individual petals.

YOU WILL NEED

- **Drops Alpaca 4ply, 100% alpaca (183yd/167m per 50g ball): 1 x 50g ball in 9034 Rose Petal (A), 2915 Dusty Orange (B), 3620 Red (C) and 7815 Forest Mix (D)**
- **Stylecraft Special DK, 100% acrylic (323yd/295m per 100g ball): A small amount of 1054 Walnut (E)**
- **3mm (UK 11:US –) crochet hook**
- **3.5mm (UK 9:US E/4) crochet hook**
- **Tapestry needle**
- **Small bag of rice or lentils**
- **Polyester stuffing**
- **A strand of black yarn**
- **2 x ⅛in (4mm) black safety eyes**
- **Chenille wire**

FINISHED SIZE

The flower head is approximately 2¾in (7cm) wide. The flower on the stem is approximately 5in (12.5cm) tall.

TECHNIQUES

Magic ring	**dc2inc**
Chain (ch)	**dc2tog**
Slip stitch (sl st)	**Half treble (htr)**
Double crochet (dc)	

PETAL BASE

Using 3mm hook and A, make a magic ring.
Round 1: 1 ch, 7 dc into the centre of the ring, join with a sl st.
Round 2: (Dc2inc) 7 times (14 sts).
Round 3: 4 ch, miss dc at base of ch and next dc, (1 htr, 2 ch, miss 1 dc) rep 5 times, sl st in top of 2nd ch (7 ch sps).
Round 4: 5 ch, (1 htr in top of htr of previous round, 3 ch) 6 times, sl st in top of 2nd ch (7 ch sps).
Round 5: 6 ch, (1 htr in top of htr of previous round, 4 ch) 6 times, sl st in top of 2nd ch (7 ch sps).
Round 6: 7 ch, (1 htr in top of htr of previous round, 5 ch) 6 times, sl st in top of 2nd ch (7 ch sps).
Fasten off and weave in ends.

PETALS

You will now work in the ch sps of rounds 3–6 on the petal base.
Using 3mm hook and A:
Row 1: Sl st in any ch sp from round 3, *(2 ch, sl st in ch sp) twice, sl st in next ch sp; rep from * 6 times (14 petals). Fasten off A.
Row 2: Change to B, sl st in any ch sp from round 4, *(2 ch, sl st in ch sp) 3 times, sl st in next ch sp; rep from * 6 times (21 petals). Fasten off B.
Row 3: Change to C, sl st in any ch sp from round 5, *(2 ch, sl st in ch sp) 4 times, sl st in next ch sp; rep from * 6 times (28 petals). Fasten off.
Row 4: Join with sl st in any ch sp from round 6, *(2 ch, sl st in ch sp) 5 times, sl st in next ch sp; rep from * 6 times (35 petals). Fasten off and weave in ends.

FLOWER FACE

Using 3mm hook and A, make a magic ring.
Round 1: 1 ch, 8 dc into the centre of the ring, join with a sl st.
Round 2: (Dc2inc) 8 times (16 sts).
Fasten off and leave a tail of yarn.

FLOWER BACK

Using 3mm hook and D, make a magic ring.
Round 1: 1 ch, 6 dc into the centre of the ring, join with a sl st.
Round 2: (Dc2inc) 6 times (12 sts).
Round 3: (1 dc, dc2inc) 6 times (18 sts).
Fasten off and leave a tail of yarn.

STEM

Using 3mm hook and D, 4 ch, sl st in 1st ch to create a loop.
Round 1: 1 ch, 4 dc into the centre of the loop.
Rounds 2–18: Work 17 rounds straight (4 sts).
Fasten off and leave a tail of yarn.

LEAF (MAKE 2)

Using 3mm hook and D, make a magic ring.
Round 1: 1 ch, 4 dc into the centre of the ring.
Round 2: (Dc2inc) 4 times (8 sts).
Round 3: (3 dc, dc2inc) twice (10 sts).
Round 4: (4 dc, dc2inc) twice (12 sts).
Rounds 5–6: Work 2 rounds straight.
Round 7: (4 dc, dc2tog) twice (10 sts).
Round 8: (3 dc, dc2tog) twice (8 sts).
Round 9: (Dc2tog) 4 times (4 sts).
Fasten off and leave a tail of yarn.

SOIL

Using 3.5mm hook and E, make a magic ring.
Round 1: 1 ch, 6 dc into the centre of the ring.
Round 2: 2 dc into each st (12 sts).
Round 3: (1 dc, dc2inc) 6 times (18 sts).
Round 4: (2 dc, dc2inc) 6 times (24 sts).
Round 5: (3 dc, dc2inc) 6 times (30 sts).
Round 6: (4 dc, dc2inc) 6 times (36 sts).
Rounds 7–11: Work 5 rounds straight.
Round 12: (4 dc, dc2tog) 6 times (30 sts).
Round 13: (3 dc, dc2tog) 6 times (24 sts).
Round 14: (2 dc, dc2tog) 6 times (18 sts).
Place a small bag of rice or lentils in the base and then stuff firmly with polyester stuffing.
Round 15: (1 dc, dc2tog) 6 times (12 sts).
Round 16: (Dc2tog) 6 times (6 sts).
Using a tapestry needle, weave this yarn through the last dc sts of the round and gather hole together. Fasten off and weave in ends.

MAKING UP

Using the photograph as a guide, place the plastic eyes and stitch the mouth on the face using black yarn. Sew the face on the front of the flower.

Turn your flower over so the back is facing you. Fold a chenille wire in half and then feed this through the middle of the flower stem. Position the stem so that it meets the centre back of the flower. Place the flower back over the top of the stem. Use the yarn tail to whip stitch (see page 122) the flower back to the back of the petals.

Poke the stem into the centre of the soil. Sew the base of the leaf to the base to the stem approximately ¾in (2cm) below the flower. With a few small stitches, sew the base of the stem to the top of the soil. Place into a small pot (see pages 124–5).

FUNKY FERN

The fern is the coolest of the house plants, with its fine green fronds flowing over the pot like hair.

YOU WILL NEED

- Drops Alpaca 4ply, 100% alpaca (183yd/167m per 50g ball): 1 x 50g ball in 2916 Bright Lime (A)
- Stylecraft Special DK, 100% acrylic (323yd/295m per 100g ball): 1 x 100g ball in 1841 Cornish Blue (B), 1001 White (C) and 1054 Walnut (D)
- 3mm (UK 11:US –) crochet hook
- 3.5mm (UK 9:US E/4) crochet hook
- Polyester stuffing
- 2 x ⅜in (10mm) safety eyes
- A strand of black yarn
- A small piece of cardboard

FINISHED SIZE

The plant in its pot is approximately 5in (12.5cm) tall and 5in (12.5cm) wide. The longest leaf is approximately 5in (12.5cm) long.

TECHNIQUES

Magic ring
Chain (ch)
Slip stitch (sl st)
Double crochet (dc)
dc2inc
dc2tog
Back loop only (blo)

NOTE

The plant leaves are worked in rows. You will work one side of the leaf, then the other side. You then attach the leaves to a ball of soil. So that the soil does not show through the pot too much, the lower half of the soil is made in white yarn and the top is then worked in the brown. You can place this plant in any pot, but I have created a nice round pot with a cheeky face.

SMALL LEAF (MAKE 2)

Row 1: Using 3mm hook and A, 17 ch.

Row 2 (First side): Sl st in 2nd ch from hook, 2 sl st, (1 sl st, 4 ch, 1 sl st in 2nd ch, 2 sl st in ch, 1 sl st in foundation ch at base of the frond) twice, (1 sl st, 5 ch, 1 sl st in 2nd ch, 3 sl st in ch, 1 sl st in foundation ch at the base of the frond) 3 times, (1 sl st, 6 ch, 1 sl st in 2nd ch, 4 sl st in ch, 1 sl st in foundation ch at the base of the frond) 3 times, (1 sl st, 7 ch, 1 sl st in 2nd ch, 5 sl st in ch, 1 st in foundation ch at the base of the frond) 5 times (13 fronds).

Now work on the other side of the foundation chain. Missing the last 3 ch sts of the foundation ch, work in the opposite side of the last st you worked in.

Row 3 (Second side): (1 sl st, 7 ch, 1 sl st in 2nd ch, 5 sl st in ch, 1 sl st in foundation ch at the base of the frond) 5 times, (1 sl st, 6 ch, 1 sl st in 2nd ch, 4 sl st in ch, 1 sl st in foundation ch at the base of the frond) 3 times, (1 sl st, 5 ch, 1 sl st in 2nd ch, 3 sl st in ch, 1 sl st in foundation ch at the base of the frond) 3 times, (1 sl st, 4 ch, 1 sl st in 2nd ch, 2 sl st in ch, 1 sl st in foundation ch at the base of the frond) twice (26 fronds).

Fasten off and weave in ends.

LARGE LEAF (MAKE 3)

Row 1: Using 3mm hook and A, 22 ch.

Row 2 (First side): Sl st in 2nd ch from hook, 2 sl st, (1 sl st, 4 ch, 1 sl st in 2nd ch, 2 sl st in ch, 1sl st in foundation ch at the base of the frond) twice, (1 sl st, 5 ch, 1 sl st in 2nd ch, 3 sl st in ch, 1 sl st in foundation ch at the base of the frond) 3 times, (1 sl st, 6 ch, 1 sl st in 2nd ch, 4 sl st in ch, 1 sl st in foundation ch at the base of the frond) 3 times, (1 sl st, 7 ch, 1 sl st in 2nd ch, 5 sl st in ch, 1 sl st in foundation ch at the base of the frond) 3 times, (1 sl st, 8 ch, 1 sl st in 2nd ch, 6 sl st in ch, 1 sl st in foundation ch at the base of the frond) 3 times, (1 sl st, 9 ch, 1 sl st in 2nd ch, 7 sl st in ch, 1 sl st in foundation ch at the base of the frond) 4 times (18 fronds).

Now work on the other side of the foundation chain. Missing the last 3 ch sts of the foundation ch, work in the opposite side of the last st you worked in.

Row 3 (Second side): (1 sl st, 9 ch, 1 sl st in 2nd ch, 7 sl st in ch, 1 sl st in foundation ch at the base of the frond) 4 times, (1 sl st, 8 ch, 1 sl st in 2nd ch, 6 sl st in ch, 1 sl st in foundation ch at the base of the frond) 3 times, (1 sl st, 7 ch, 1 sl st in 2nd ch, 5 sl st in ch, 1 sl st in foundation ch at the base of the frond) 3 times, (1 sl st, 6 ch, 1 sl st in 2nd ch, 4 sl st in ch, 1 sl st in foundation ch at the base of the frond) 3 times, (1 sl st, 5 ch, 1 sl st in 2nd ch, 3 sl st in ch, 1 sl st in foundation ch at the base of the frond) 3 times, (1 sl st, 4 ch, 1 sl st in 2nd ch, 2 sl st in ch, 1 sl st in foundation ch) at the base of the frond twice (36 fronds).

Fasten off and weave in ends.

SOIL

Using 3.5mm hook and D, make a magic ring.

Round 1: 1 ch, 6 dc into the centre of the ring.

Round 2: 2 dc into each st (12 sts).

Round 3: (1 dc, dc2inc) 6 times (18 sts).

Round 4: (2 dc, dc2inc) 6 times (24 sts).

Round 5: (3 dc, dc2inc) 6 times (30 sts).

Round 6: (4 dc, dc2inc) 6 times (36 sts).

Rounds 7–12: Work 6 rounds straight.

Fasten off D and change to C.

Round 13: (4 dc, dc2tog) 6 times (30 sts).

Round 14: (3 dc, dc2tog) 6 times (24 sts).

Round 15: (2 dc, dc2tog) 6 times (18 sts).

Stuff firmly with polyester stuffing.

Round 16: (1 dc, dc2tog) 6 times (12 sts).

Round 17: (Dc2tog) 6 times (6 sts).

Using a tapestry needle, weave this yarn through the last dc sts of the round and gather hole together. Fasten off and weave in ends.

POT

Using 3.5mm hook and B, make a magic ring.

Round 1: 1 ch, 8 dc into the centre of the ring.

Round 2: 2 dc into each st (16 sts).

Round 3: (1 dc, dc2inc) 8 times (24 sts).

Round 4: (2 dc, dc2inc) 8 times (32 sts).

Round 5: Work 1 round (32 sts).

Round 6: Work 1 round blo (32 sts).

Round 7: (3 dc, dc2inc) 8 times (40 sts).

Round 8: Work 1 round (40 sts).

Round 9: (4 dc, dc2inc) 8 times (48 sts).

Round 10: Work 1 round (48 sts).

Round 11: (5 dc, dc2inc) 8 times (56 sts).

Fasten off B.

Rounds 12–16: Change to C. Work 5 rounds straight. Fasten off C.

Round 17: Change to B. (5 dc, dc2tog) 8 times (48 sts).

Round 18: Work 1 round (48 sts).

Round 19: (4 dc, dc2tog) 8 times (40 sts).

Round 20: Work 1 round (40 sts).

Round 21: (3 dc, dc2tog) 8 times (32 sts).

Round 22: Work 1 round blo (32 sts).

Fasten off and weave in ends.

MAKING UP

Arrange the three large leaves in the centre of the soil and then place the small leaves in between. Sew securely to the centre of the soil. Using the photograph as a guide, place the plastic eyes and stitch the mouth using black yarn.

Place a small piece of cardboard (about 2¼in/6cm in diameter) in the base of the pot. Put a little bit of stuffing in the base of the pot. Pop the plant with its soil into the pot and arrange the fronds of the fern around the features to resemble hair.

CUTE FLOWER BASKET

This basket, filled with a huge bunch of pretty flowers, makes a wonderful gift or just a little token to cheer someone up. I have sewn on a few gold beads in the centre of the flowers to bring a little extra sparkle to the crochet.

YOU WILL NEED

- **Sirdar Haworth Tweed DK, 50% nylon, 50% wool (180yd/165m per 50g ball): 1 x 50g ball in 910 Harewood Chestnut (A)**
- **Rico Ricorumi DK, 100% cotton (63yd/58m per 25g ball): 1 x 25g ball in 010 Smokey Rose (B), 005 Vivid Vanilla (C), 013 Raspberry (D), 019 Mauve (E) 034 Denim (F), 035 Midnight Blue (G), 076 Marsh Green (H) and 057 Chocolate (J)**
- **3.5mm (UK 9:US E/4) crochet hook**
- **Polyester stuffing**
- **Tapestry needle**
- **2 x 5⁄16in (8mm) safety eyes**
- **Some 1⁄8in (3mm) gold pearl beads**
- **Cotton thread**
- **A strand of black yarn**
- **A small piece of cardboard**

FINISHED SIZE

The basket with handle is approximately 3in (7.5cm) wide and 5in (12.5cm) tall.

TECHNIQUES

Magic ring	dc2tog
Chain (ch)	Treble stitch (tr)
Slip stitch (sl st)	Half treble (htr)
Double crochet (dc)	Back loop only (blo)
dc2inc	

NOTE

The basket is worked in worked in rounds from the base up, using a spiral linen stitch. Especially when working the sides of the basket, place a marker at the beginning of each round so you know where you are in the pattern. You might be tempted to chain 2 sts at the beginning of round 7, but stick with the pattern. By simply using 1 chain, you will avoid a large hole. The top of the basket is then made and attached to the sides. The flowers and leaves are then attached to the top.

BASKET

Using 3.5mm hook and A, make a magic ring.

Round 1: 1 ch, 8 dc into the centre of the ring.

Round 2: 2 dc into each st (16 sts).

Round 3: (dc2inc, 1dc) 8 times (24 sts).

Round 4: (2 dc, dc2inc) 8 times (32 sts).

Round 5: 1 dc, dc2inc, (3 dc, dc2inc) 7 times, 2 dc (40 sts).

Round 6: 1 dc in each st blo (40 sts).

Round 7: Place marker, 1 ch, miss st at base of ch, dc in next st, (1 ch, miss 1 st, dc in next st) rep to marker (40 sts).

Rounds 8–15: (1 ch, miss 1 st, dc in next st) around (40 sts).

Round 16: 1 dc blo in each st (40 sts).

Fasten off and weave in ends.

HANDLE

Using 3.5mm hook and A, 31 ch.

Row 1: Sl st in 2nd ch from hook, sl st to end (30 sts).

Row 2: Now work along the other side of the ch sts, 1 ch, sl st in each ch to end (30 sts).

Fasten off and leave an 8in (20cm) tail of yarn.

BASKET TOP

Using 3.5mm hook and J, make a magic ring.
Round 1: 1 ch, 8 dc into the centre of the ring.
Round 2: 2 dc into each st (16 sts).
Round 3: (Dc2inc, 1 dc) 8 times (24 sts).
Round 4: (2 dc, dc2inc) 8 times (32 sts).
Round 5: 1 dc, dc2inc, (3 dc, dc2inc) 7 times, 2 dc (40 sts).
Rounds 6–7: Work 2 rounds straight.
Fasten off and leave a long tail of yarn.

FLOWER

(MAKE 8 IN VARIOUS COLOURS)

Using 3.5mm hook and B, 5 ch, sl st in 1st ch to make a loop.
Round 1: Sl st in next st, *(2 htr, 1 tr, 2 htr, sl st) in same st, sl st in next st; rep from * 4 times (5 petals).
Fasten off and leave a tail of yarn.

LEAF (MAKE 6)

Using 3.5mm hook and H, 5 ch.
Row 1: 1 dc in 2nd ch from hook, (1 htr, 1 tr) in next ch, (1 tr, 1 htr) in next ch, (1 htr, 1 dc) in last ch, 1 ch. Now turn and work down the other side of the foundation ch: (1 dc, 1 htr) in 1st ch, (1 htr, 1 tr) in next ch, (1 tr, 1 htr) in next ch, (1 dc, 1 sl st) in 1st ch.
Fasten off and leave a tail of yarn.

MAKING UP

Using the photograph as a guide, place the plastic eyes and stitch the mouth using black yarn. Place a small piece of cardboard (about 3in/7.5cm in diameter) in the base of the basket. Firmly stuff the basket. Place the basket top on the top of the stuffing and whip stitch (see page 122) the basket and top together. Sew the ends of the handle to the top of the basket. Sew three small beads in the centre of each flower. Place the flowers and leaves on the basket and then sew securely to the top of the basket. Weave in all ends.

SWEET WATERING CAN

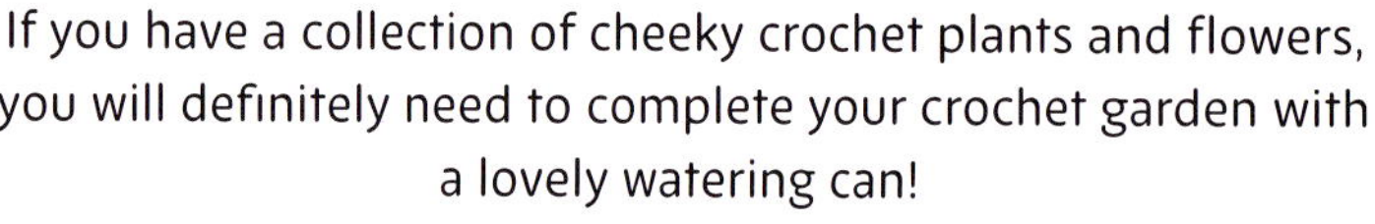

If you have a collection of cheeky crochet plants and flowers, you will definitely need to complete your crochet garden with a lovely watering can!

YOU WILL NEED

- Scheepjes Catona, 100% mercerized cotton (137yd/125m per 50g ball): 1 x 50g ball in 074 Mercury (A), a small amount of 110 Jet Black (B), 280 Lemon (C) and 106 Snow White (D)
- 3.5mm (UK9:USE/4) crochet hook
- Polyester stuffing
- Tapestry needle and stitch marker
- A pair of ⅜in (10mm) safety eyes
- A strand of black yarn
- A small piece of cardboard
- Chenille stick and floristry wire

FINISHED SIZE

The watering can is approximately 6in (15cm) wide (measurement includes spout and handle) and 4in (10cm) tall.

TECHNIQUES

Magic ring
Chain (ch)
Slip stitch (sl st)
Double crochet (dc)
dc2inc
dc2tog
Treble stitch (tr)
Back loop only (blo)
Crab stitch

NOTE

The watering can is worked in rounds from the base up, using the standard amigurumi technique. The black inside of the watering can is then made and attached to the sides using a whip stitch. A half lid is then folded in half and sewn on top. Place a marker at the beginning of each round so you know where you are in the pattern.

WATERING CAN

Using 3.5mm hook and A, make a magic ring.
Round 1: 1 ch, 8 dc into the centre of the ring.
Round 2: Dc2inc into each st (16 sts).
Round 3: (Dc2inc, 1 dc) 8 times (24 sts).
Round 4: (2 dc, dc2inc) 8 times (32 sts).
Round 5: 1 dc, dc2inc, (3 dc, dc2inc) 7 times, 2 dc (40 sts).
Round 6: (Dc2inc, 4 dc) 8 times (48 sts).
Round 7: 1 dc in each st blo (48 sts).
Rounds 8–20: Work 13 rounds straight.
Round 21: Work round in crab st.
Fasten off and weave in ends.

INSIDE AND CAN TOP

(MAKE 2: 1 X A AND 1 X B)

Using 3.5mm hook and B, make a magic ring.
Round 1: 1 ch, 8 dc into the centre of the ring.
Round 2: Dc2inc into each st (16 sts).
Round 3: (Dc2inc, 1 dc) 8 times (24 sts).
Round 4: (2 dc, dc2inc) 8 times (32 sts).
Round 5: 1 dc, dc2inc, (3 dc, dc2inc) 7 times, 2 dc (40 sts).
Round 6: (Dc2inc, 4 dc) 8 times (48 sts).
Rounds 7–8: Work 2 rounds straight.
Fasten off and leave a long tail of yarn.

TOP HANDLE

Using 3.5mm hook and A, 31 ch.
Row 1: 1 dc in 2nd ch from hook, dc to end, turn (30 sts).
Rows 2–3: Work 2 rows straight.
Fasten off and leave an 8in (20cm) tail of yarn.

SIDE HANDLE

Using 3.5mm hook and A, 15 ch.
Row 1: 1 dc in 2nd ch from hook, dc to end, turn (14 sts).
Rows 2–3: Work 2 rows straight.
Fasten off and leave an 8in (20cm) tail of yarn.

SPOUT

Using 3.5mm hook and A, make a magic ring.
Round 1: 1 ch, 5 dc into the centre of the ring.
Round 2: Dc2inc into each st (10 sts).
Rounds 3–10: Work 8 rounds straight.
Round 11: 1 dc, 3 htr, 6 dc (10 sts)
Fasten off and leave an 8in (20cm) tail of yarn.

FLOWER

Using 3.5mm hook and C, make a magic ring.
Round 1: 1 ch, 5 dc into the centre of the ring.
Fasten off C.
Round 2: Change to D, join with a sl st, *(2 ch, 4 tr, 2 ch, sl st) in same st, sl st in next st; rep from * 4 times, sl st to join (5 petals).

MAKING UP

Using the photograph as a guide, place the plastic eyes and stitch the mouth using black yarn. Place a chenille stick inside the spout. Using the tail of yarn, sew the last round of the spout to the side of the can, making sure the htr sts are at the base of the spout.

Place a small piece of cardboard (around 3in/7.5cm in diameter) in the base of the watering can. Firmly stuff the can. Sew the inside circle to the inside of the can using a whip stitch. Then fold the can top in half and sew along one edge.

Weave floristry wire through the WS stitches of the top and side handle. Attach the short edges to the side of the can using small sewing stitches. Sew the flower to the inside of the can.

GETTING STARTED

All the tools and materials you will need to use to create your cute crocheted plants are explained here, along with essential know-how on abbreviations and conversions.

TIP You can use any yarn you like for these projects. I have used both 4ply and DK weight with either a 3mm or 3.5mm hook. But you could create mini versions using a sock yarn or lace-weight yarn and 2.5mm hook, or go gigantic and create a huge cactus with a super chunky yarn and 9mm–15mm hook. I warn you, though: chunky yarns are physically quite demanding to work with. You will feel as if you have done a full workout!

CROCHET HOOKS

Crochet hooks come in a range of materials and sizes. In this book, depending on the thickness of the yarn, I use either a 3mm or 3.5mm ergonomic metal-pointed crochet hook.

YARN

I love to work in a range of yarns, from the most expensive merino for soft baby blankets through to hard-wearing cottons for toys and homeware. The key issue with making cute items is to find a yarn which has a vibrant colour or replicates the tones of the plants and flowers. For items that will be played with, cotton is always a good option as it can easily be cleaned.

Nowadays yarn producers sell yarns in dainty 10g or 25g quantities, which are perfect for small projects like these, but you certainly don't have to go out and buy special balls of yarn. Please do use yarn in your stash if you can. I have quoted the yarn I have used for these patterns, but when I want to make a gift for a friend, I will go fossicking around in my yarn collection to find something suitable. If you have a small amount of green variegated yarn in the bottom of a project bag, this will be ideal for a realistic leaf.

ACRYLIC AND FASHION YARNS

For some of the items I have used small balls of polyester chenille yarn. This has a very fluffy texture and is great for making super-cute toys. It is not very easy to see where the stitches are, so I use my fingers to find the next gap where the hook should go.

STUFFING

I have used Minicraft Supersoft toy stuffing to stuff the plants. This material complies with BS145, BN5852 and EN71 standards and is safe for children. Make sure plants are stuffed so that they are firm but not bulging, as you don't want to distort the look of the overall plant.

WEIGHTING YOUR PLANT DOWN

In some cases it is a good idea to take an old sock or a stocking and put a small amount of rice or lentils in the toe. Tie it off and use this to weight down the soil. Fill up the rest of the soil with stuffing. This little bit of weight will help your flower stems stay upright.

PLASTIC SAFETY EYES

Most of the plants in this book have plastic safety eyes. They come in two parts: the eye with a shank to push through the crochet and then a plastic washer which fits very securely over the shank inside the item. One the washer has been added it is very hard to dismantle. My advice is to make sure you have placed your eyes where you want them. Perhaps even fill the item with a little stuffing to ensure the eyes are in the right position before you attach the washers. Once you have pushed both parts of the eyes together, give them a tug test: try to pull them out so you can make sure they are fixed securely. The craft company Rico also produces a small button eye that is very effective and is good for flat items like the Mini Monstera plant (see page 32).

NEEDLES

You will need sewing needles to complete the projects, including a tapestry needle for sewing in ends and adding details.

WIRE

On a number of items I have used some floristry wire for stalks. I have also used craft chenille-covered wire 'pipe cleaners'. Using wire in items that children might play with is not a good idea. Only use wire if the item is ornamental. In every case, make sure the wire is not poking out of your plant so it does not hurt you or any inquisitive admirer of your work.

TIP Even experienced crocheters need to check that they have the correct number of stitches or rows. I don't use expensive stitch markers; I just cut a small amount of yarn, about 2in (5cm) long, and place this between the last stitch of one row and the first stitch of the next row. When I have finished, these small strands can easily be pulled out without snagging the stitches.

ABBREVIATIONS

blo	back loop only
ch	chain
ch sp	chain space
cm	centimetre(s)
dc	double crochet
dc2inc	double crochet into the next stitch (increase by one stitch)
dc2tog	double crochet two stitches together (decrease by one stitch)
dec	decrease
DK	double knitting
dtr	double treble
flo	front loop only
g	gram(s)
htr	half treble
in	inch(es)
inc	increase
m	metre(s)
mm	millimetre(s)
rep	repeat
RS	right side
Rtrf	raised treble front
Rtrb	raised treble back
sl st	slip stitch
sp	space
st(s)	stitch(es)
tog	together
tr	treble
tr2tog	treble crochet two stitches together (decrease by one stitch)
yd	yard(s)
WS	wrong side
x-dc	cross double crochet

UK AND US DIFFERENCES

Some UK and US terms have different meanings, which can cause confusion so always check which style your pattern uses. This will ensure that your crochet develops correctly. There is nothing more frustrating than working on a pattern, then realizing it is all wrong and needs to be unravelled. This book is written in UK crochet terms.

UK crochet terms	US crochet terms
Double crochet	Single crochet
Half treble	Half double crochet
Treble	Double crochet
Double treble	Triple crochet

CONVERSIONS

Crochet hook sizes

UK	Metric	US
14	2mm	–
13	2.25mm	B/1
12	2.5mm	–
–	2.75mm	C/2
11	3mm	–
10	3.25mm	D/3
9	3.5mm	E/4
–	3.75mm	F/5
8	4mm	G/6
7	4.5mm	7
6	5mm	H/8
5	5.5mm	I/9
4	6mm	J/10
3	6.5mm	K/10.5
2	7mm	–
0	8mm	L/11
00	9mm	M–N/13
000	10mm	N–P/15

CROCHET TECHNIQUES

In this section you can learn the basic techniques needed for the projects in this book. Some will need a bit of practice, but once you have learnt them you can add texture and decoration to all your cute crocheted plants.

HOLDING A HOOK

Hold your hook in either your right or your left hand as you would a pen, in between your index finger and thumb.

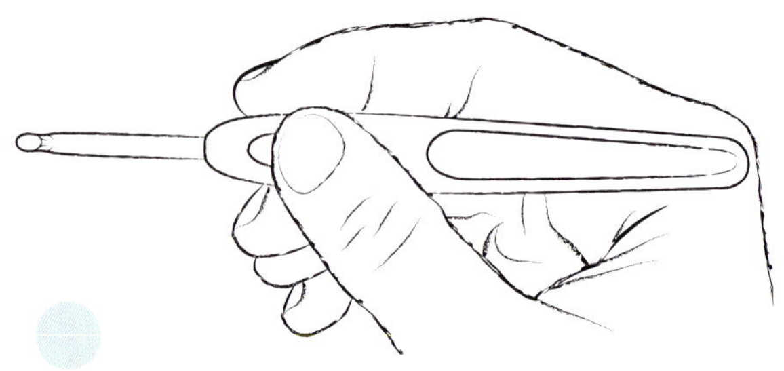

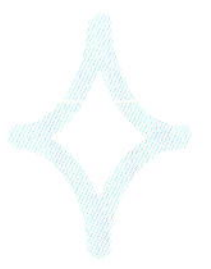

HOLDING YARN

With the hand you are not using to hold the hook, wrap the yarn around your little finger and then drape the yarn over your hand. You can hold the tail of your yarn between the middle finger and your thumb and use your index finger to control the yarn.

MAKING A SLIP KNOT

Make a loop of yarn over two fingers. Pull a second loop through this first loop, pull it up and slip it onto your crochet hook. Pull the knot gently so that it forms a loose knot on the hook.

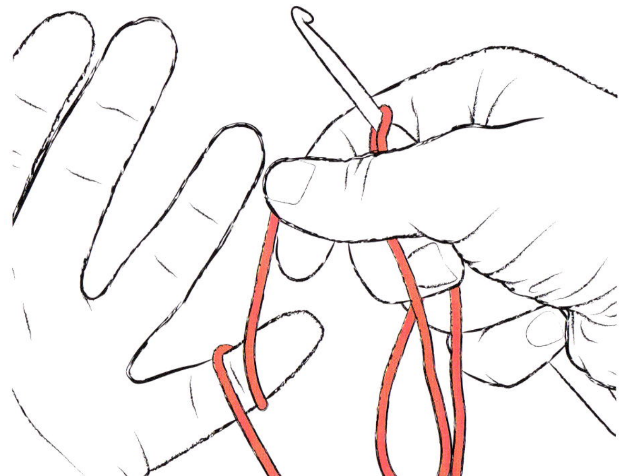

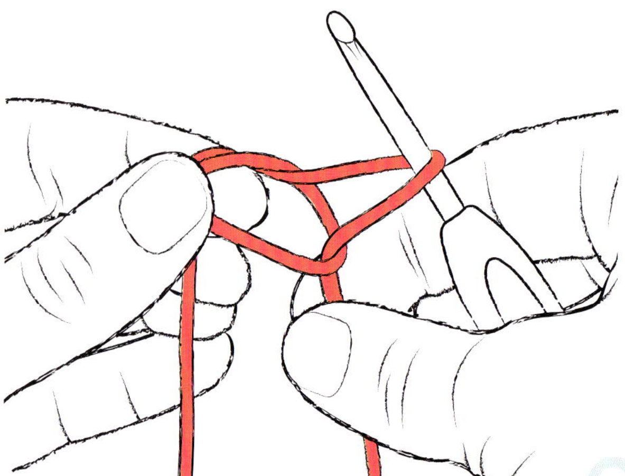

CHAIN (CH)

1. Start with a slip knot on the hook.

2. Wrap the yarn over the hook.

3. Pull the loop through the loop of the slip knot to form one chain stitch.

1.

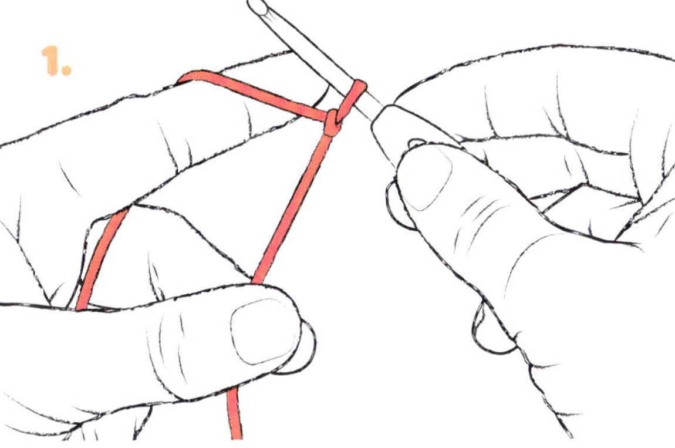

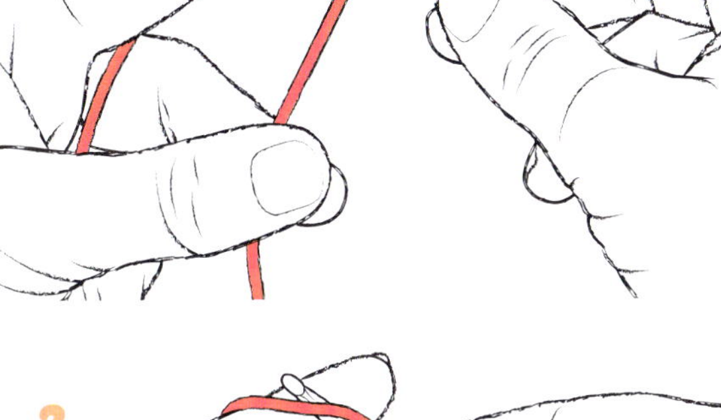

2.

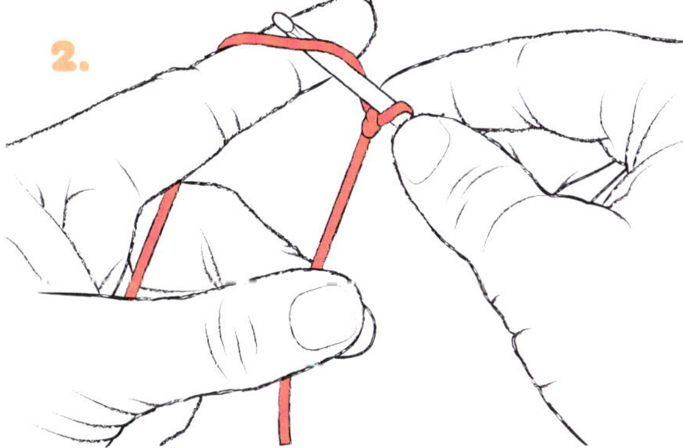

3.

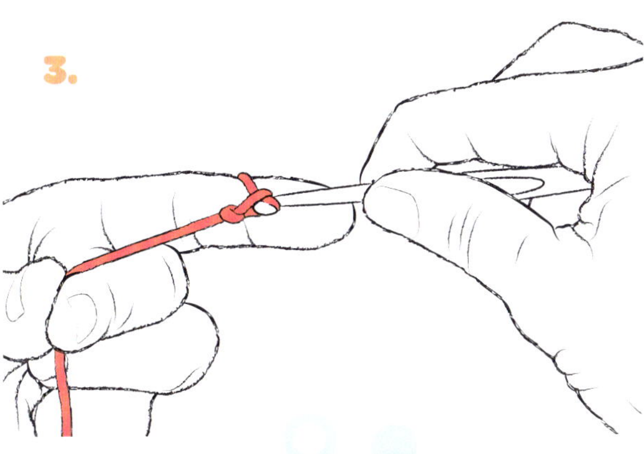

SLIP STITCH (SL ST)

This stitch is ideal for decoration and for attaching two pieces of crochet together.

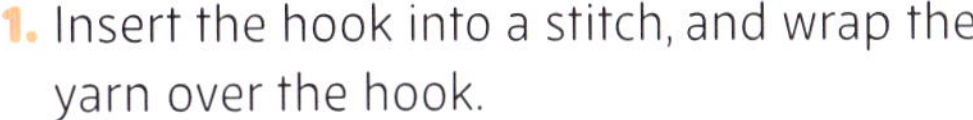

1. Insert the hook into a stitch, and wrap the yarn over the hook.

2. Draw the loop through the stitch and the loop on the hook. Continue in this way for the required number of slip stitches.

1.

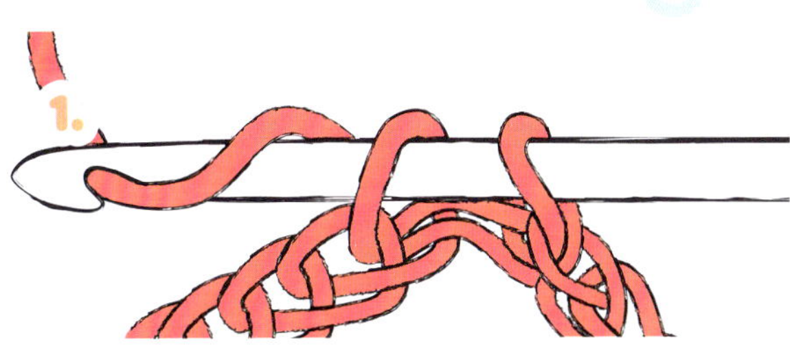

2.

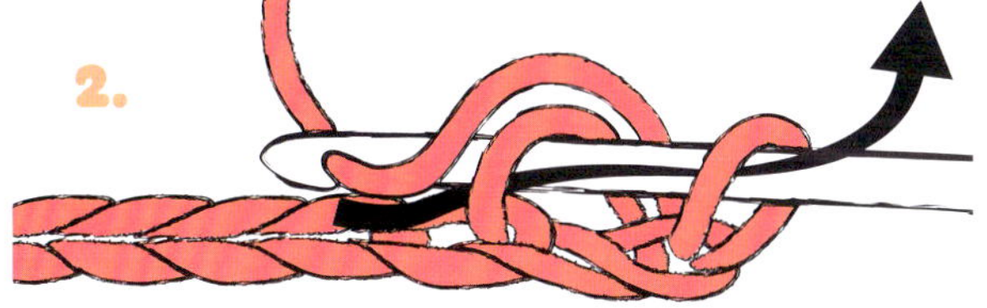

DOUBLE CROCHET (DC)

1. Insert the hook through the stitch, yarn over the hook, and pull through the stitch. There will be two loops on the hook.

2. Wrap the yarn over the hook and pull through both loops on the hook. There will be one loop on the hook.

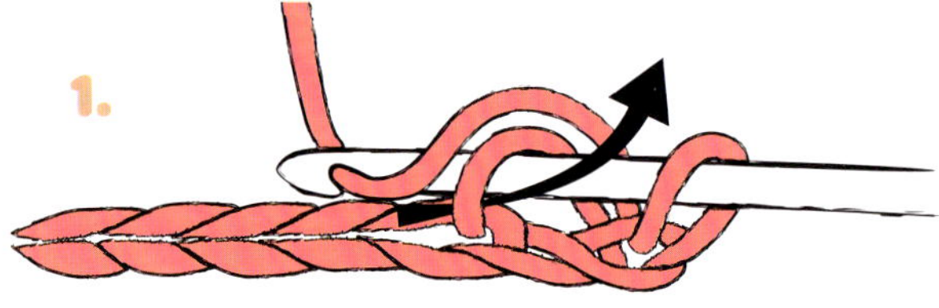

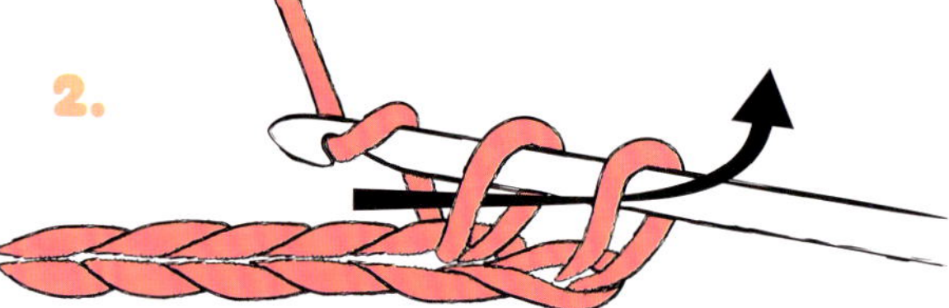

CROSS DOUBLE CROCHET (X-DC)

This technique is used to make the flower centre of the Sunflower (see page 68), the Cuddly Christmas Tree (see page 54) and the Soft Christmas Wreath (see page 50).

1. Insert the hook through the stitch, yarn under the hook, and pull through the stitch. There will be two loops on the hook.

2. Wrap the yarn over the hook and pull through both loops on the hook. There will be one loop on the hook.

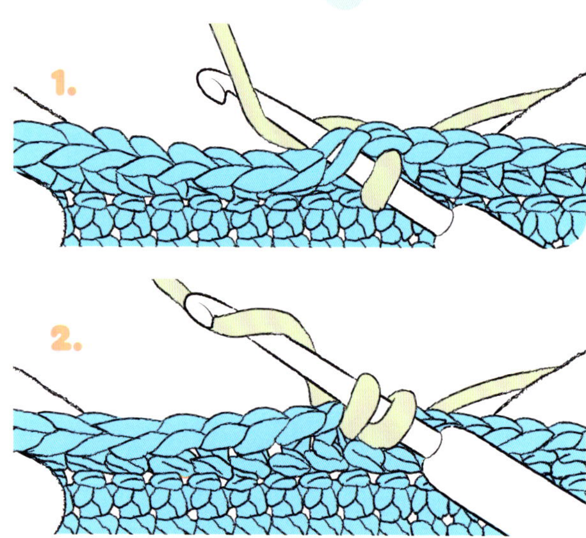

HALF TREBLE (HTR)

1. Wrap the yarn over the hook, insert the hook through the stitch, yarn over the hook and pull through the stitch. There will be three loops on the hook.

2. Wrap the yarn over the hook again and draw through all the loops on the hook. There will be one loop on the hook.

TREBLE CROCHET (TR)

1. Wrap the yarn over the hook, and insert the hook through the stitch. Wrap the yarn over the hook and pull through the stitch.

2. Wrap the yarn over the hook and pull through two loops. There will be two loops on the hook.

3. Wrap the yarn over the hook again and pull through the remaining two loops. There will be one loop left on the hook.

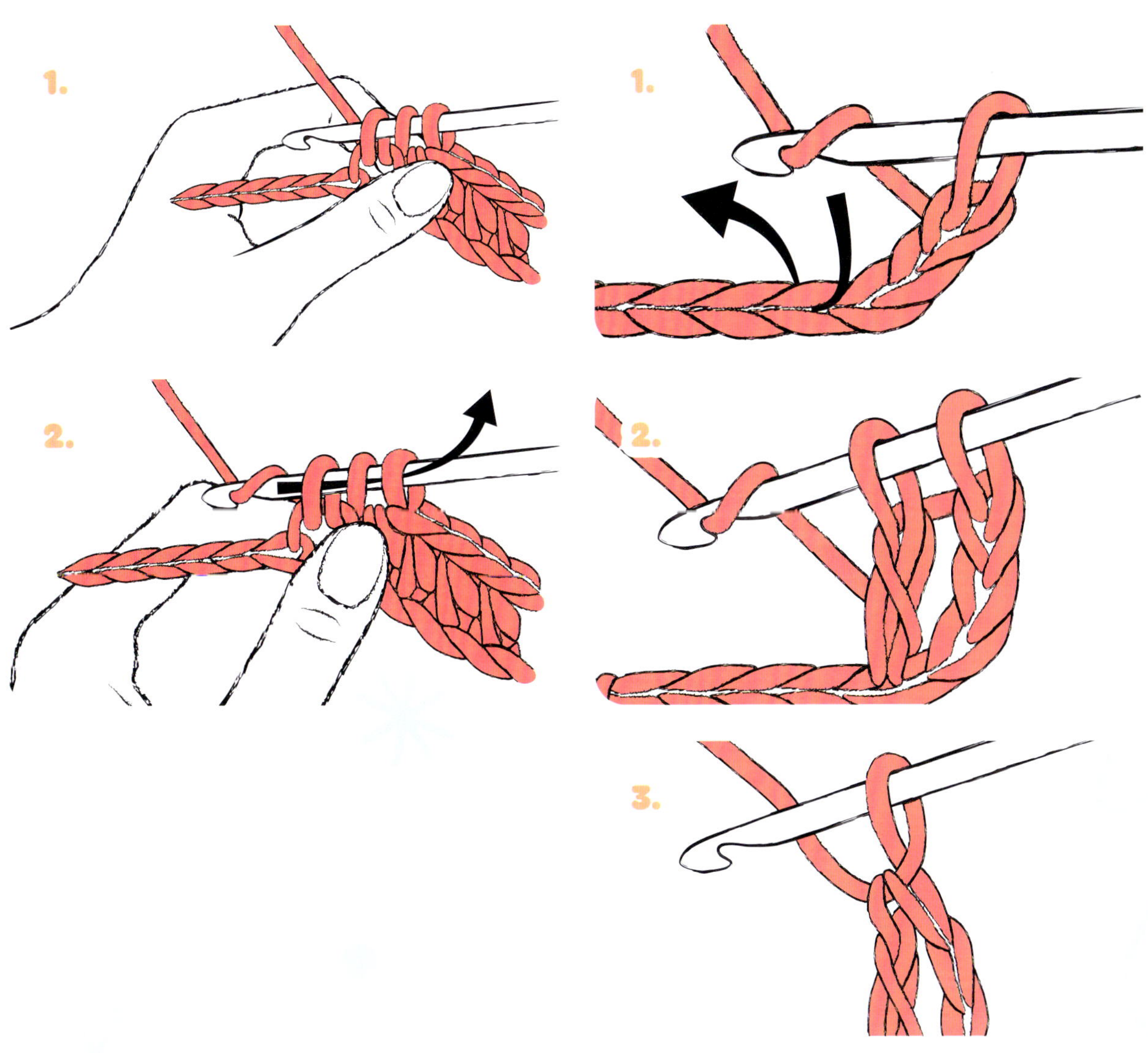

DOUBLE TREBLE (DTR)

1. Wrap the yarn over the hook twice, insert the hook through the stitch, yarn over the hook and pull through the stitch. There will be four loops on the hook.

2. Wrap the yarn over the hook and pull through two loops. There will be three loops on the hook.

3. Wrap the yarn over the hook and pull through two loops. There will be two loops on the hook.

4. Wrap the yarn over and pull through the remaining two loops. There will be one loop on the hook.

1.

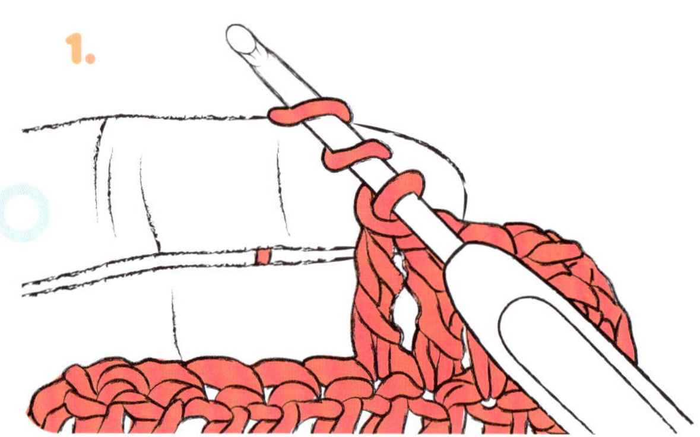

3.

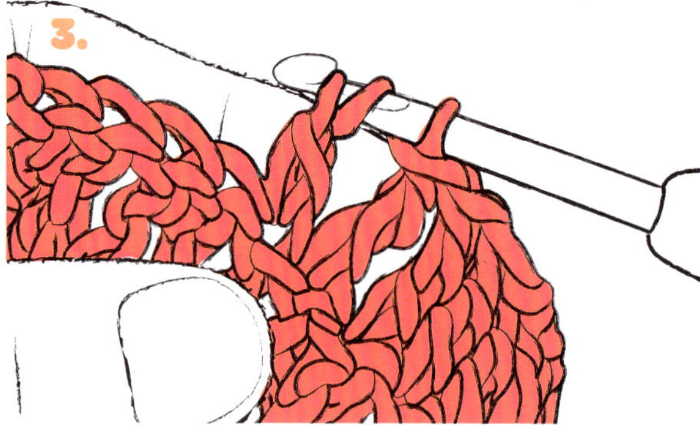

2.

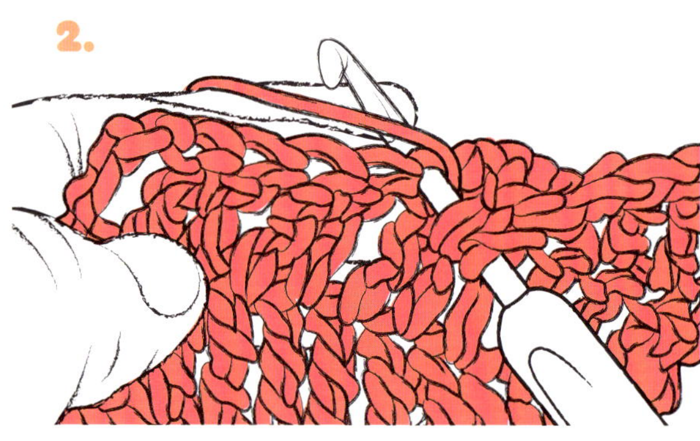

4.

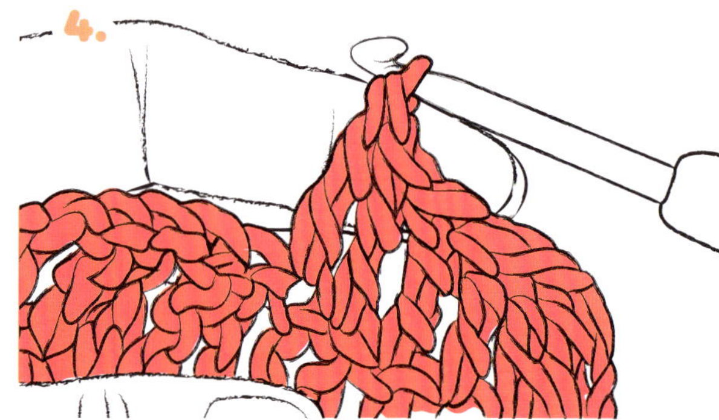

WORKING IN ROWS

When making straight rows, you need to make a turning chain at the beginning of the row for the stitch you are working on. A double crochet row will need one chain at the beginning of the row; this will be indicated in the pattern.

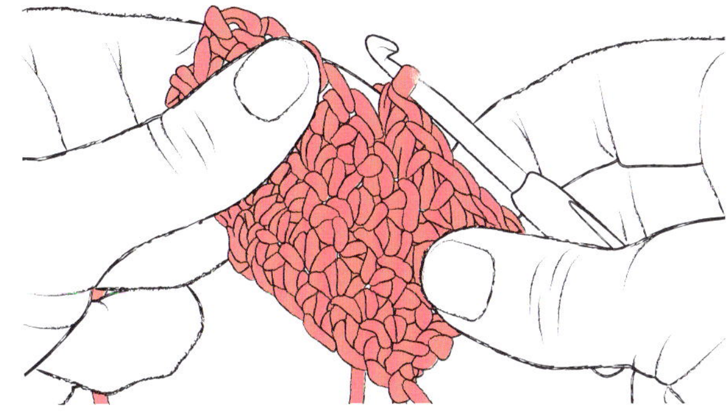

WORKING IN ROUNDS

One wonderful thing about crochet is that you don't always have to work in rows; you can also work in rounds. The majority of the patterns in this book are worked in rounds, beginning with a magic ring. They are worked using the 'amigurumi' crochet technique, crocheting in a continuous spiral with no slip-stitch joins or turning chains. In this way you can create one seamless cyclindrical shape.

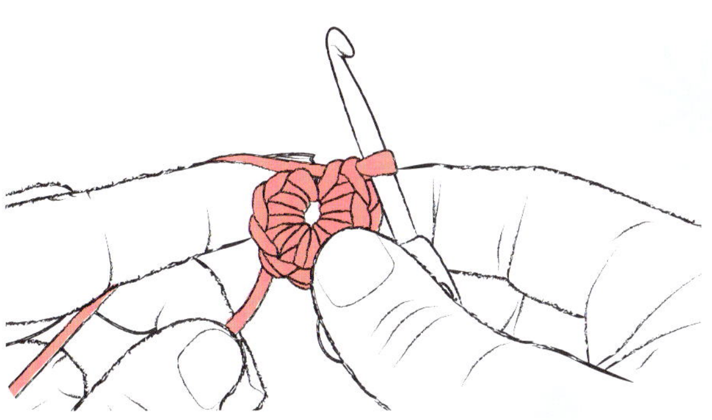

In order to know where each round starts it is advisable to place a marker at the beginning of each round.

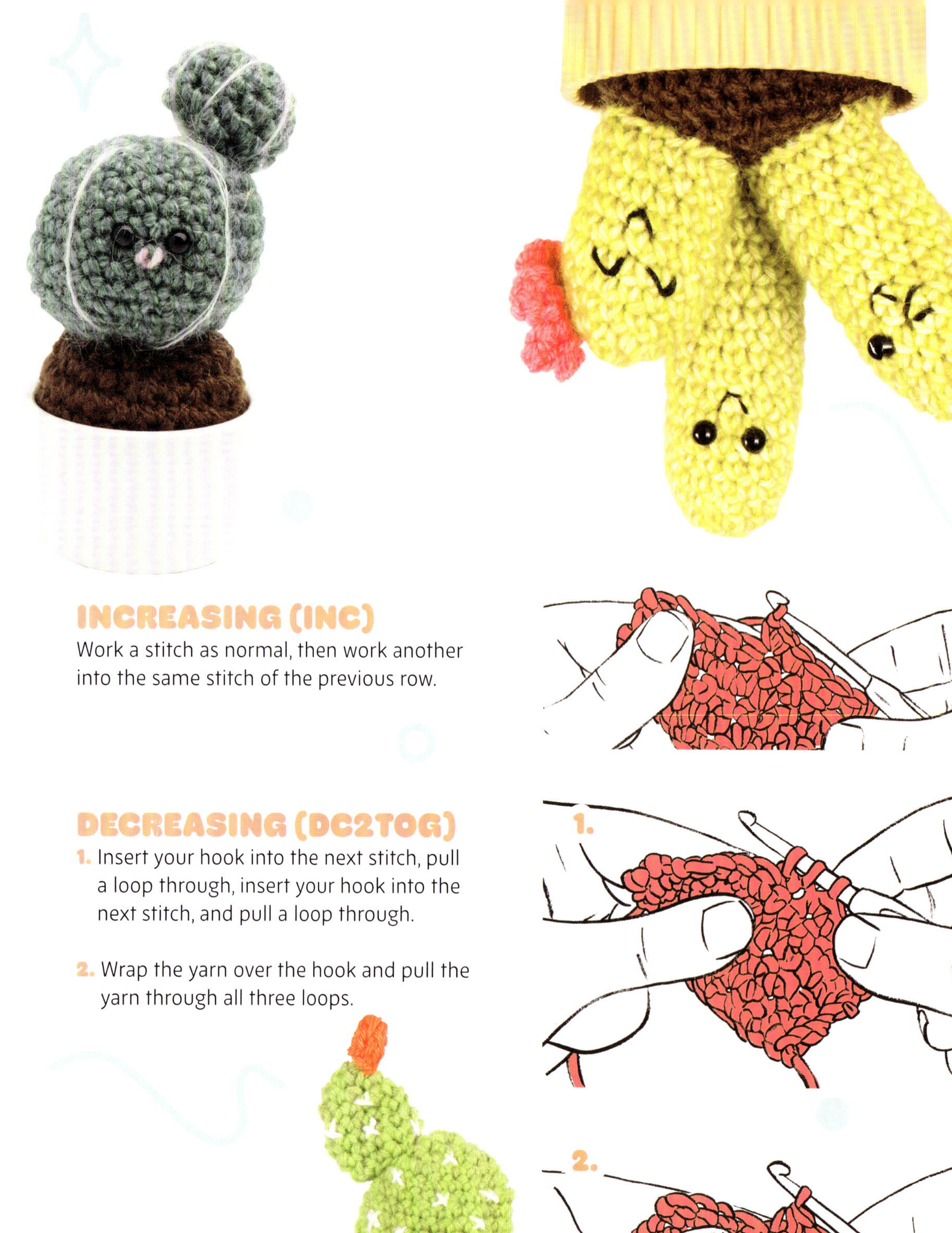

INCREASING (INC)

Work a stitch as normal, then work another into the same stitch of the previous row.

DECREASING (DC2TOG)

1. Insert your hook into the next stitch, pull a loop through, insert your hook into the next stitch, and pull a loop through.

2. Wrap the yarn over the hook and pull the yarn through all three loops.

BOBBLE

The String of Pearls pattern (see page 40) creates a bobble by drawing several htr stitches together and then making a sl st in the first ch of the stitch.

1. Work the number of chain stitches specified in the instructions for your pattern.
2. Make 3 htr stitches in the first ch, yarn over.
3. Pull through all four loops on the hook.
4. Sl st in the first ch made at the beginning of the stitch.

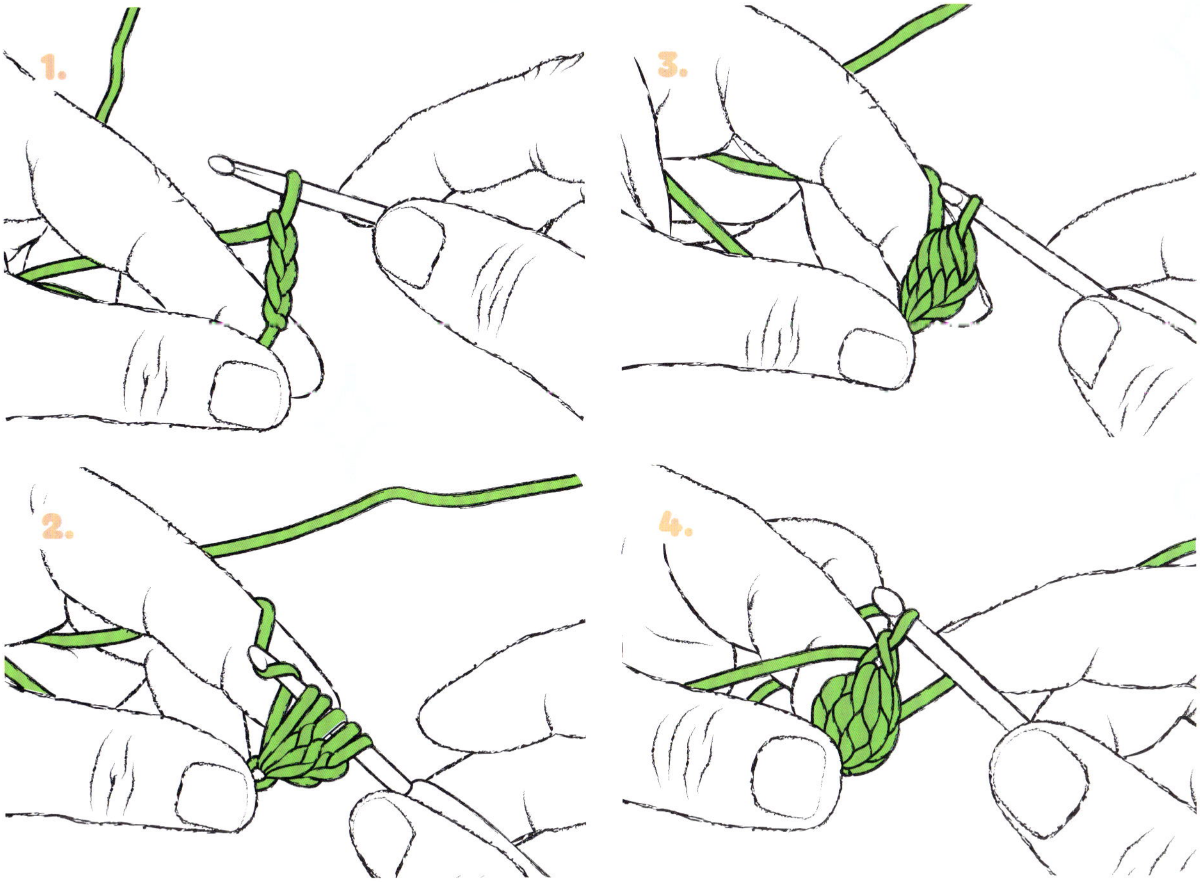

1.

3.

2.

4.

MAGIC RING

A very clever way to start an amigurumi shape is to use a 'magic ring'. This is a neat way of starting a circular piece of crochet while avoiding the unsightly hole that can be left in the centre when you join a ring the normal way. Magic rings are nearly always made with double crochet stitches, as this creates a tight, dense crochet fabric.

1. Start by making a slip knot. Pull up the loop and slip this loop onto your crochet hook.

2. Before you tighten the ring, wrap the yarn over the hook (outside the circle) and pull through to make the first chain.

3. Insert the hook into the ring, wrap the yarn over the hook and pull through the ring so there are two loops on the hook.

4. Wrap the yarn over the hook again (outside the circle) and pull through both loops.

5. You have made your first double crochet stitch.

6. Continue to work like this for as many double crochet stitches as are stated in the pattern instructions.

7. Pull the yarn tail to tighten the ring and then continue working in the round as usual.

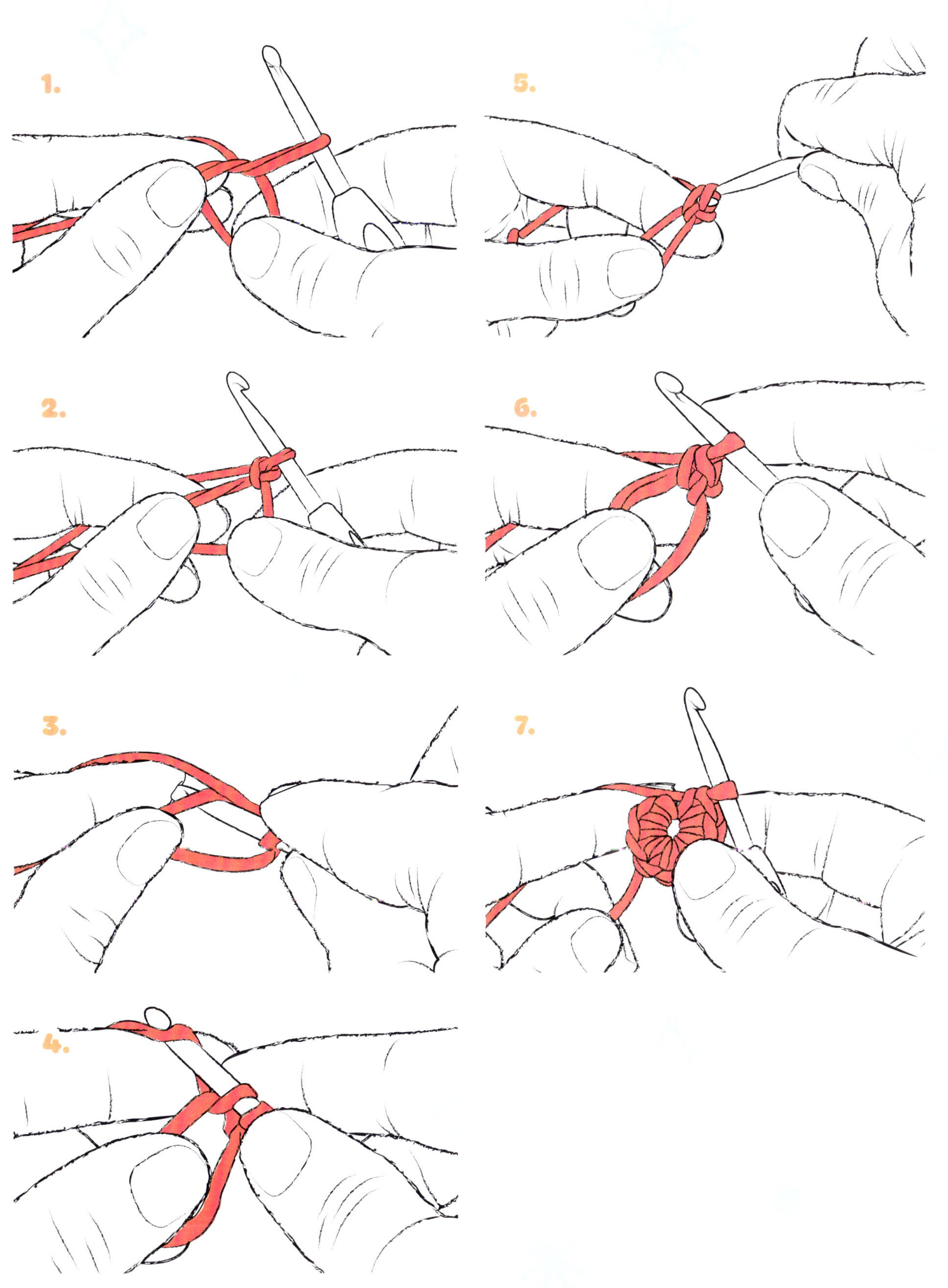
1.
2.
3.
4.
5.
6.
7.

WORKING IN THE BACK LOOP ONLY (BLO)

Generally, a crochet stitch is made by slipping the hook under the top two loops of a stitch. However, you can also create a different effect by working into the back loop only of each stitch of one round or row. This creates a ridge or horizontal bar across the row. In this book I have used this technique for several projects in this book, including the Tropical Tall Cactus (see page 18). You can also work in the front loop only (flo).

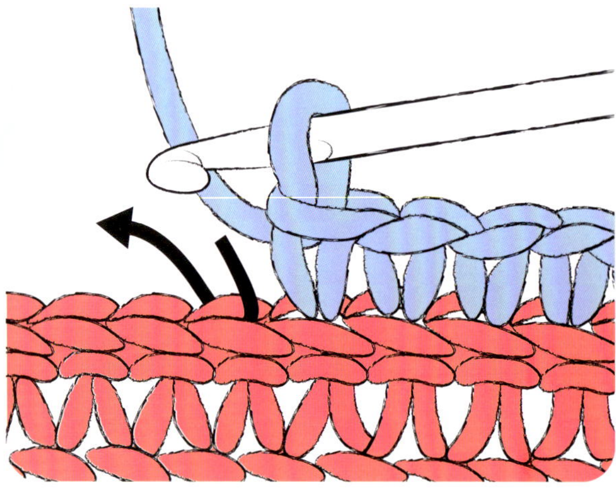

CRAB STITCH

Crab stitch gives a neat finish, creating the effect of a corded edge. I have used this technique for the edge of the Snake's Tongue plant (see page 46). It is made by working double crochet in the opposite direction from normal, that is, from left to right. It can feel slightly awkward to work but is worth persevering with.

1. With RS facing, insert the hook from front to back into the stitch immediately to the right of the last one. Point the hook slightly downward and catch the yarn at the back. Bring the yarn through the stitch. Wrap the yarn round the hook and draw it through the two loops.

2. Repeat to the end of the row.

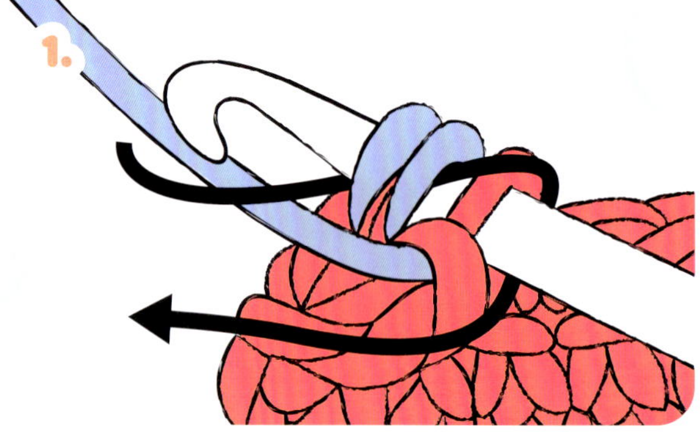

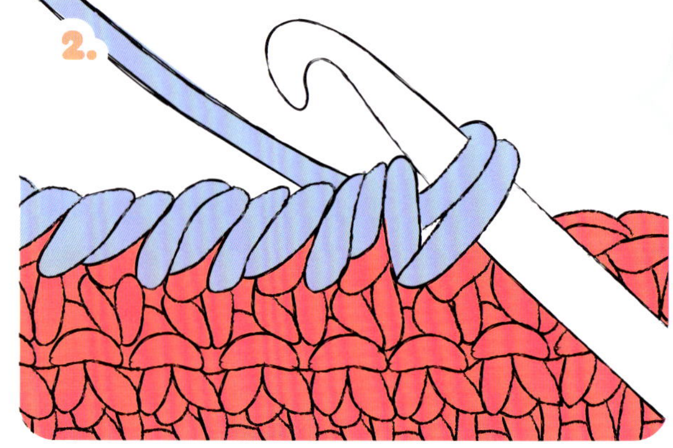

RAISED TREBLE FRONT (RTRF)

This is a brilliant technique for creating texture and gives a ribbed effect that I have used for the Mexican Ball Cactus (see page 24). You work your crochet hook around the stitches created on the previous row.

1. Wrap the yarn over the hook and insert your hook from front to back around the post of the next stitch.

2. Wrap the yarn over the hook and pull through two loops. There will be two loops on the hook.

3. Wrap the yarn over the hook again and pull through the remaining two loops. There will be one loop left on the hook.

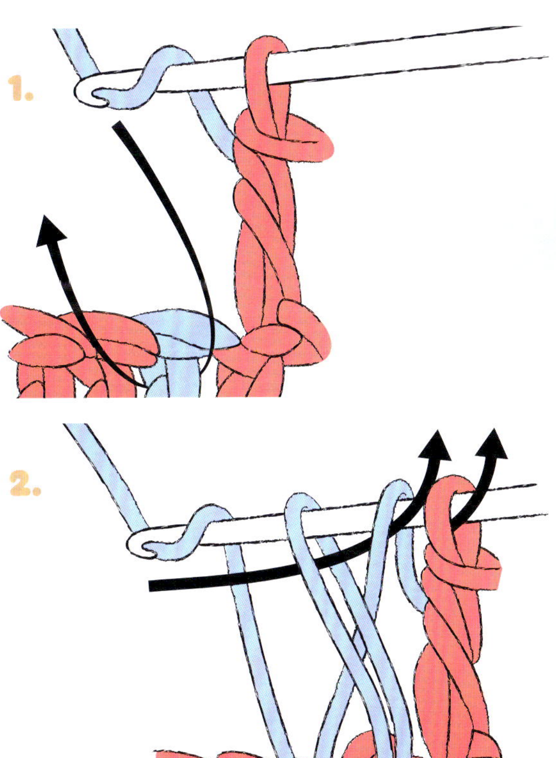

RAISED TREBLE BACK (RTRB)

This is a partner stitch to the raised front treble stitch. You can create a deeper rib effect by alternating both these stitches, and I have done this with the Mexican Ball Cactus (see page 24). The method is worked in exactly the same way as Rtrf (left) except that in step 1 you insert your hook from the back to the front.

FINISHING TOUCHES

This section shows you how to make up your finished project so that it is robust and durable. I have used embroidery techniques to give the plants and flower faces extra detail. You will need a tapestry needle and some yarn to sew these stitches on the surface of your piece; if you have never done any embroidery before, why not make a small square of double crochet and practise first?

BACK STITCH

Back stitch is excellent for creating a straight line and creating the expression of the mouth. Using the illustration as a guide, bring your needle up through the fabric at A and then push the needle back down at B, bring the needle up again at C, and then down again at A. Work like this to create a neat, continuous line.

FRENCH KNOT

If you are not using safety eyes, French knots are ideal for sewing eyes or dots onto your flower or plant face. Bring your needle up through the fabric and then wrap your thread around the needle three times. Then insert the needle back into the fabric very close to where it emerged.

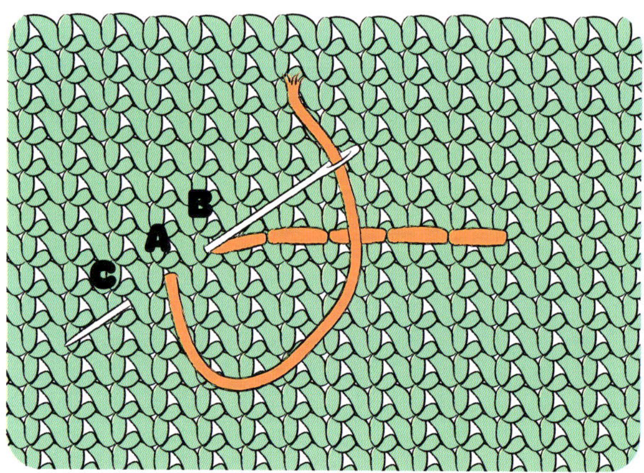

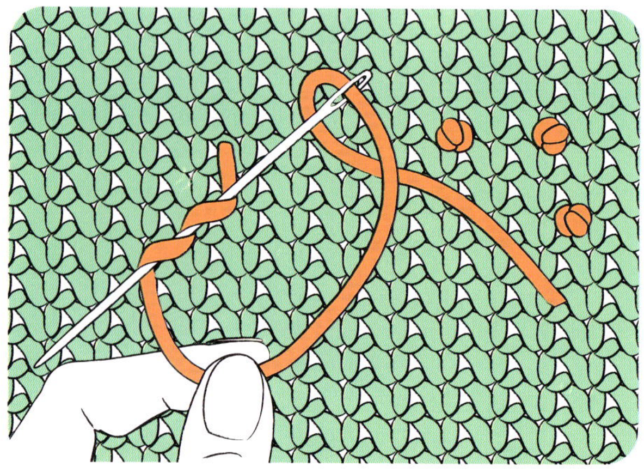

WINDING YARN ROUND WIRE

You may prefer to cover the wire you use by winding the yarn around it. If this is the case, cut the wire to the length of the stem you require. Tightly wind the yarn around the stem. Leave about a 3in (7.5cm) tail of yarn which you can use to sew the stem to the back of the flower. Secure the ends with a small amount of fabric glue and leave to dry.

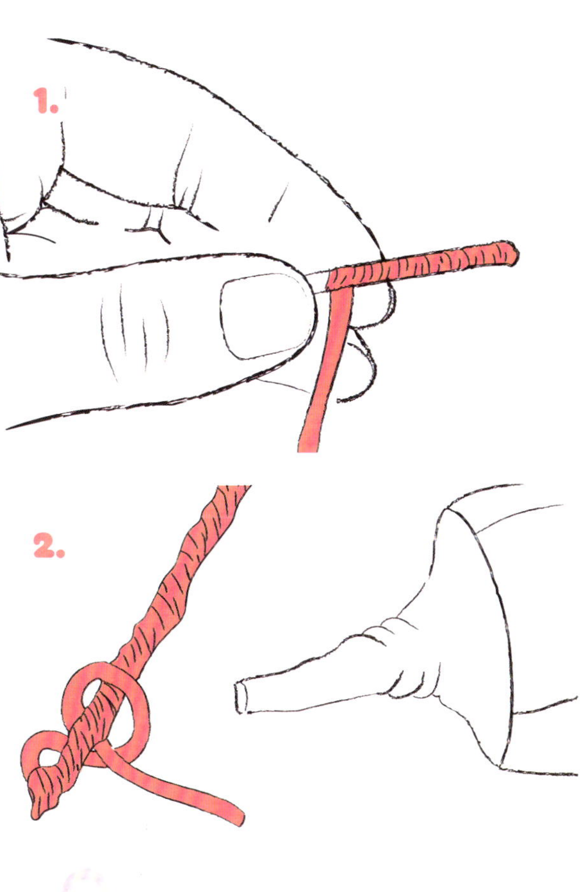

WEAVING IN ENDS

Try to leave about 8in (20cm) of yarn when you fasten off. You might use it to join the flower to a leaf or stem. I always ensure that my ends have been woven backwards and forwards three times.

1. Thread the remaining yarn end onto a blunt tapestry needle and weave in the yarn on the wrong side of the project. Work along the stitches one way, then work back in the opposite direction.

2. Weave the needle behind the first ridge of crochet for at least 2in (5cm). Snip off the end of the yarn close to the fabric of the crochet.

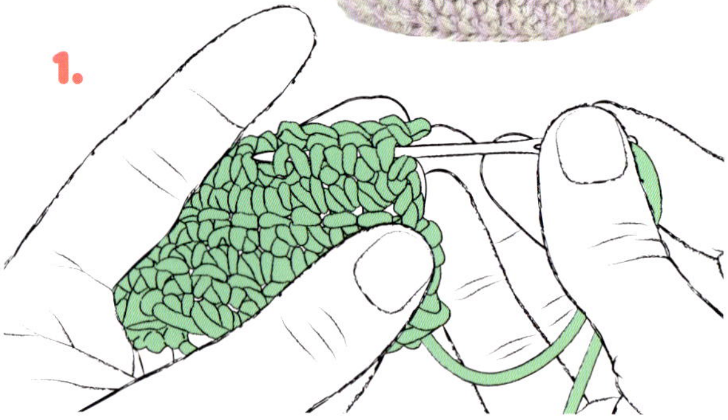

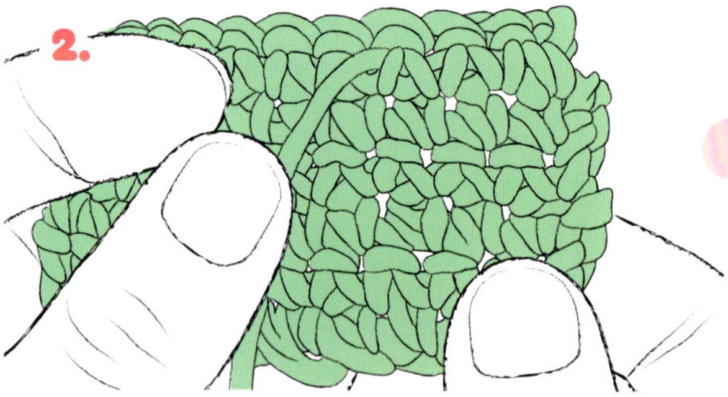

WHIP STITCH

You can use whip stitch to sew two layers of fabric together. Make a knot at the end of your yarn. Bring your tapestry needle from the wrong side through to the right side of your fabric, then hold both pieces of your fabric together, wrong sides facing each other. Push your needle from the back piece through to the front piece, and repeat evenly along the edge. There will be a row of small stitches along the edge of your work, joining both pieces together.

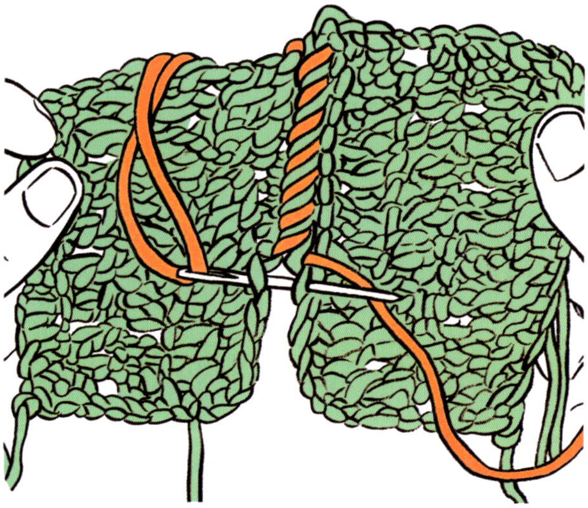

MAKING A POMPOM WITH A FORK

I love to use a pompom maker, but the projects like the Mexican Ball Cactus (see page 24) need a much thinner, flatter one to replicate the spiky plant flowers. The best way to create these flowers is to dive into the cutlery drawer and pull out a faithful fork.

1. Cut a piece of yarn about 12in (30cm) long and place this on the side of the tines.
2. Wrap the yarn around the fork about 10 times.
3. Knot the piece of yarn that you have along the side of the fork.
4. Cut the wool loop on the other side of the fork.
5. Trim your yarn to create a flat pompom.

CROCHETED POTS

You can source plant pots to display your finished projects, but you could also crochet a pot, and choose colours to complement both the plant and your decor. I find it useful to add some structure by covering a cardboard pot used for seedlings.

NOTE

Each pot is worked in spirals using the standard amigurumi technique (see page 113).

YOU WILL NEED

PLAIN POT

- **Stylecraft Life DK, 75% acrylic, 25% wool (326yd/298m per 100g ball): 1 ball in 2448 Bark (A), or any colour you like**

FUNKY POT

- **Rico Essentials Cotton DK, 100% cotton (142yd/130m per 50g ball):**
  1 ball in 14 Fuchsia (A)
  1 ball in 80 White (B)

BOTH POTS

- **3mm (UK 11:US –) crochet hook**
- **1 x biodegradable (cardboard) pot 2¼in (6cm) in diameter**
- **Craft glue**

FINISHED SIZE

The pot is approximate 2¼in (6cm) in diameter at the top, 2in (5cm) in diameter at the bottom and 2¼in (6cm) high.

PLAIN POT

Using 3mm hook and A, make a magic ring.
Round 1: 1 ch, 8 dc into the centre of the ring.
Round 2: 2 dc into each st (16 sts).
Round 3: (1 dc, dc2inc) 8 times (24 sts).
Rounds 4–5: Work 2 rounds straight.
Round 6: Work 1 round blo (24 sts).
Round 7: (2 dc, dc2inc) 8 times (32 sts).
Rounds 8–9: Work 2 rounds straight.
Round 10: (3 dc, dc2inc) 8 times (40 sts).
Rounds 11–12: Work 2 rounds straight.
Round 13: (4 dc, dc2inc) 8 times (48 sts).
Rounds 14–18: Work 5 rounds straight.
Rounds 19–20: Work 2 rounds blo (48 sts).
Fasten off and weave in ends.

FUNKY POT

Using 3mm hook and A, make a magic ring.
Round 1: 1 ch, 8 dc into the centre of the ring.
Round 2: 2 dc into each st (16 sts).
Round 3: (1 dc, dc2inc) 8 times (24 sts).
Rounds 4–5: Work 2 rounds straight.
In the next row and every following row, work with the two colours, leaving a strand of the colour you are not using just above your work so that it is captured by the yarn you are working. Place a marker at the beginning of each round.
Round 6: (3 dc blo in A, 3 dc blo in B) 4 times (24 sts).
Round 7: (3 dc in A, 3 dc in B) 4 times (24 sts).
Round 8: (2 dc, dc2inc in A, 2 dc, dc2inc in B) 4 times (32 sts).
Rounds 9–10: (4 dc in A, 4 dc in B) 4 times (32 sts).
Round 11: (3 dc, dc2inc in A, 3 dc, dc2inc in B) 4 times (40 sts).
Rounds 12–15: (5 dc in A, 5 dc in B) 4 times (40 sts).
Rounds 16–17: Fasten off B and work 2 rounds in A.
Rounds 18–19: Work 2 rounds blo (40 sts).
Fasten off and weave in ends.

MAKING UP

Cover the outside of the cardboard pot with some craft glue. Carefully pull the crochet over the pot, making sure the top of the crocheted pot covers the cardboard. Leave to dry.

ACKNOWLEDGEMENTS

Thank you to the wonderful team at GMC. They have a passion and dedication to ensure your craft books are the very best and I am fortunate to work with them. Thank you to my editor Sara and also to Jonathan Bailey, the publisher who trusts me to come up with appealing projects. Thanks must also go to Andrew Perris for the photography, and Robin Shields and Ellie Smith for the design and illustration. Thank you also to Jude Roust who did such a great job checking the patterns, and to Alexis Harvey for copy editing the text.

I would like to thank a number of yarn producers and retailers for their support. Thanks to Stylecraft Ltd and the team at Spa Mill, Annabelle and Juliet, who generously donated many of the yarns that I use in the projects.

I continue to love and enjoy the support and encouragement of my crafty best friends Lucy (Attic 24) and Christine (Winwick Mum) – they believe I have a yarn time machine to make all this crazy stuff in.

I am grateful that my family joins me in laughing and getting excited by the mad things I create: Benjamin, Robert and the very important 'mews', Stanley.

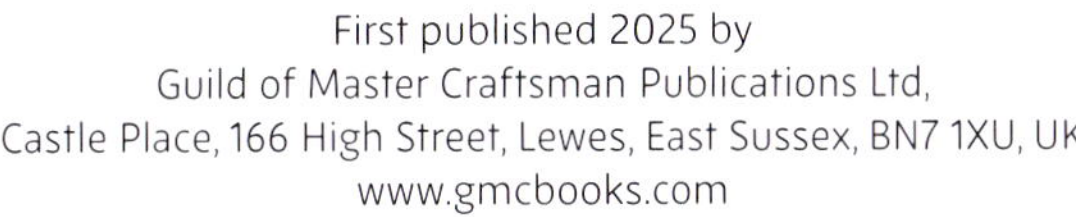

First published 2025 by
Guild of Master Craftsman Publications Ltd,
Castle Place, 166 High Street, Lewes, East Sussex, BN7 1XU, UK
www.gmcbooks.com

ISBN 978 1 78494 714 9

The EEA authorised representative is Authorised Rep Compliance Ltd.
Ground Floor, 71 Baggot Street Lower, Dublin, D02 P593, Ireland
www.arccompliance.com

A catalogue record for this book is available from the British Library.

Publisher Jonathan Bailey
Production Jim Bulley
Senior Project Editor Sara Harper
Editor Alexis Harvey
Design Manager Robin Shields
Designer Ellie Smith
Pattern Checker Jude Roust
All photography by Andrew Perris, except pages 104–105
(Shutterstock.com)

Colour origination by GMC Reprographics
Printed and bound in China

To order a book, contact:
GMC Publications Ltd
Castle Place, 166 High Street,
Lewes, East Sussex, BN7 1XU,
United Kingdom
Tel: +44 (0)1273 488005
www.gmcbooks.com